IN GOD'S HOLY LIGHT

• • •

In
God's
Holy
Light

• • •

WISDOM
FROM THE
DESERT
MONASTICS

• • •

JOAN CHITTISTER

Franciscan
MEDIA
Cincinnati, Ohio

Excerpts from *The Sayings of the Desert Fathers: The Apophthegmata Patrum: The Alphabetic Collection* by Benedicta Ward, SLG, trans. CS 59 (Collegeville, MN: Cistercian Publications, 1975). Used by permission of Liturgical Press. All rights reserved. From *Desert Wisdom: Sayings from the Desert Fathers* by Yushi Nomura. Copyright ©1982, 2001 by Yushi Nomura. Reprinted with permission of Orbis Books, Maryknoll, New York. All Rights Reserved.

Cover and book design by Mark Sullivan
Cover image © iStock | goikmitl

Library of Congress Cataloging-in-Publication Data
Chittister, Joan.
In God's holy light : wisdom from the desert monastics / Joan Chittister.
pages cm
ISBN 978-1-61636-831-9 (alk. paper)
1. Desert Fathers. 2. Monastic and religious life of women—Middle East—History—Early church, ca. 30-600. 3. Spiritual life—Christianity—Early works to 1800. I. Title.
BR67.C46 2015
271.009'015—dc23
2015024560

ISBN 978-1-61636-831-9

Published by Franciscan Media
28 W. Liberty St.
Cincinnati, OH 45202
www.FranciscanMedia.org

Printed in the United States of America.
Printed on acid-free paper.
15 16 17 18 19   5 4 3 2

To Anne Wambach, O.S.B.,
a Benedictine woman
whose life and leadership
continues in the spirit of those
in whose spirit she walks

Contents

Chapter One

BEWARE OF BOGUS SPIRITUALITY

Once the rule was made in Scetis that they should fast for the entire week before Easter. During this week, however, some brothers came from Egypt to see Abba Moses, and he made a modest meal for them. Seeing the smoke, the neighbors said to the priests of the church of that place: "Look, Moses has broken the rule and is cooking food at his place." Then the priests said: "When he comes out, we will talk to him." When the Sabbath came, the priests, who knew Abba Moses' great way of life, said to him in public: "Oh, Abba Moses, you did break the commandment made by people, but you have firmly kept the commandment of God."

T he Desert Monastics, thousands of monks and nuns who went into the Egyptian wastelands in the third to sixth centuries, have come to be seen as the Olympians of the spiritual life. They went to the desert deliberately in order to live very close to the basics of life: no comfort food, no superfluities, no excesses. They went to separate themselves even physically from the lures of the world around them—from gluttony, debauchery, materialism, pride—and in the process they became the spiritual athletes of the time. Like the great runners or discus throwers or gladiators around them, they denied themselves the comforts of life in order to excel in the pursuit of God. They did everything they could do to eliminate the frills of life, to see and desire and listen to God alone.

It was an admirable and impressive array of people, whole cities of them like Scetis, the one mentioned in this story, clustered together and concentrated on one thing alone—on God. They devoted themselves totally to the rigors of fasting and the denial of the body in order to sharpen the sensitivities of the soul. Their lifestyle and their spiritual practices became legendary. Some of them prayed all night; others fasted all day; many of them sat alone with God all their entire lives. All of them lived lives of prayer and bodily asceticism.

They became the mystics, the spiritual directors and the counselors of the age. People flocked to the desert to hear from them a Word, a spiritual parable or maxim that would serve to guide their own lives once they returned to the city. What could be more laudatory? What's not to like about this kind of concentration on the important things of life? Answer: the possibility of satisfaction, of self-conceit.

The truth is that the danger of asceticism lies in the fact that the asceticism itself may become a substitute, a very flattering substitute, for the real spiritual life. If the purpose of asceticism is misunderstood, misplaced, or exaggerated, asceticism, at least in our time, can discolor the whole spiritual life for many. In a period of humanistic psychology, the destruction of the body—for any reason under any form—is not easily seen as a sane response to life.

So why have this story? Precisely because it is so important to our understanding of what holiness really looks like when holiness is meant to be on our minds.

In this story, the need for physical rigor as well as for rule-making and law-keeping as a sign of holiness is embedded in popular opinion. In fact, the religious watchdogs of the time go straight to religious authorities to complain about the spiritual mediocrity of one of the holiest men of the age, Abba Moses. "This one," they report, "breaks the great fast—eats with lay people!—simply because his company arrived. It's a scandal; it's a sin; do something about it."

And the equally-holy spiritual leaders of the time do: In public, on the Sabbath, they call Moses out to address the problem. Before the entire community of seekers, they confront Moses with his lapse of holy obedience to the rule. And in doing so, they confirm real spirituality in the face of bogus spirituality. "Abba Moses," they say, "you did break the commandment made by people." (Let there be no doubt: they did understand the offense.) "But," they go on, "you have firmly kept the commandment of God."

So much for human commands in the face of the commandments of God to love your neighbor, to be merciful, to feed the hungry, to give drink to the thirsty, and to be clean of heart.

The place of this story in the lexicon of the spiritual life is clear: We may not substitute the penances we do during Lent, for instance, for what we should be doing to meet the needs of the world around us. Our penances are meant to give us the spiritual and moral strength to do what needs to be done, to make life better for those who are in need around us. They are not meant to excuse us from doing it.

Chapter Two

THE WORST RELIGIOUS SIN

Abba Anthony said: "The time is coming when people will be insane, and when they see someone who is not insane, they will attack that person saying: 'You are insane because you are not like us.'"

N ever doubt for a minute that "keeping up with the Joneses" is not as much a religious phenomenon as it is an economic one. Being like the people we want to have like us is a social phenomenon of major proportions. Grounded in fear or greed, it can cause whole populations to shift social behaviors like schools of fish change direction.

Social psychologists call it "herd behavior" or the "mob mentality" and have been studying facets of it since the nineteenth century. No one knows better than economists the dangers of it now. And no small part of it happens in religion. Because some people begin to predict the end of the world, other people set calendar dates for a world catastrophe and stack their backyard bunkers with supplies enough to last for years. Worse still, religious madness may well be more engrained in social thought than other social ills. The witch burnings in the United States—the executions of women for "consorting with the devil"— completely belie the very founding ideals of the country. Suppression of religious freedom throughout the world exposes the grain of ignorance that runs through every society that claims concern about God. The attacks on churches in the Middle East, the tribal wars in Africa, the laws of exclusion that followed the great wars of religion in Europe right up to the twentieth century, are clear proof that we all have sinned. We name "difference" madness and make mad attempts to stamp out the other.

But the Desert Monastics, the most "catholic" of Catholics in an age of pristine revelation, would have none of it. Abba Anthony brooks no doubt: Exclusion in the name of God is the very worst of religious sins. God speaks in many tongues and to every color and age of people. It is not ours to decide where God's favor lies.

But it is ours to see as a spiritual task the obligation to come to our own opinions. We are not to buy thought cheaply. We are not to attach ourselves to someone else's decisions like pilot fish and simply go with the crowd. We are meant to be thinking Christians.

Religious persecution of blacks and Irish and Protestants and women and gays and Muslims, just because it is the tenor of the time, is to our eternal shame. To make these things acts of faith, which we have over time, all of us and each of us, is the greatest infidelity to our Creator God. It is the very kind of rejection that ranged against Jesus. He was a Galilean. And he had the gall to speak up for Canaanites and lepers and women and Samaritans and the poor and the stranger in the land. He refused to bow to the social pressure that comes with being "other." So they cast him out of the pale of his religion; or, like Nicodemus, snuck in to see him only at night; or in the square called, "Crucify him, crucify him, crucify him!"

And Jesus left to all of us the obligation to speak up on issues that threaten to erode our humanity. To speak out for the innocent and oppressed. To speak on, however long it takes and whatever the pressures ranged against us. To speak up when we hear around us the strategies of those who would balance the national budget by denying the hungry food stamps, and children good education, and the unemployed and underpaid decent lives, and the strangers in the land a way to become community.

Our obligation is not to be like those who would secure themselves by making others insecure. Our obligation is to be like Jesus. And that is anything but insane.

Chapter Three

WHAT JESUS WANTS

Some old men came to see Abba Poemen, and said to him: "Tell us, when we see brothers dozing during the sacred office, should we pinch them so they will stay awake?" The old man said to them: "Actually, if I saw a brother sleeping, I would put his head on my knees and let him rest."

T he seductive thing about any kind of ascetic practices— giving up candy, eating fish instead of meat, going to weekday masses, saying a rosary everyday—is that they're measurable. You can count them. People can see you doing them. At very least, there is a kind of personal satisfaction, a sense of achievement, a comfort, that comes from knowing that we're really doing something to make ourselves holier people. Athletes do the same thing. They count push-ups, aerobic exercises, and the number of miles they cycle on a bike. And that's good. But those things are not all that the spiritual life is about, if they are even a small part of it. It's easy to count duties done, yes, but sense of justice, not so much; charity, even less. The core values of the spiritual life are as much about the attitudes that underlie the way we go about life as they are about the regularity of our devotions.

The spiritual tragedy lies in the fact that we can say fifty Hail Marys a day and at the same time do nothing for the family next door who can't pay their electric bill in the wintertime, let alone advocate for changes in the welfare laws. We can go to daily Mass and then go home and pad our income tax forms. We can give up meat on Fridays forever and stay racist. We can give away all our old coats to the local clothing drive for the poor and still do nothing about equal pay for women who are now 40 percent of the primary wage earners in the country.

Or better yet, we can use our own pious practices as a benchmark with which to judge—and find wanting—the religious disciplines of others. As in this story of Abba Poemen's in which the temptation is, oh, so clearly, a human pastime, regardless of the eighteen centuries between then and now.

Regular pious practices, as important as they are to the awakening of spiritual consciousness in us, are not what the spiritual life is really about. In fact, those very practices may become an obstacle to our full spiritual development. And that is not new news. Abba Poemen knew it in the third century, and did not shrink at the effort it would take to school people in the truth of it—even those who thought they already were spiritual.

With this story, legalism and false asceticism pale in the light of greater virtue. What Abba Poeman calls for here is the godliness of mercy and compassion and forgiveness: the very holiness that pious practices are meant to sow in us and that rigidity for its own sake can never substitute. Nor does our failure to be unwaveringly faithful to the practice of them count against the value of those whose hearts are right even when their knees are weak. The number of people who have made Lenten resolutions over the centuries and then, in despair of perfection, gave up doing them after they broke them once, should have known Abba Poeman.

In the spiritual life, we are meant to prod our souls to regular discipline so that in doing so our hearts will be softened to serve those whom Jesus served. The gentle Jesus wants clean hearts from us, not sacrifice; deep down basic commitment, not simply blue ribbons for winning the spiritual marathons we've run to make ourselves feel holy.

Chapter Four

THE PERILS OF PRIVATE OWNERSHIP

Abba Evagrius said that there was a brother, called Serapion, who didn't own anything except the Gospel, and
this he sold to feed the poor. And he said these words,
which are worth remembering: "I have even sold the
very word which commanded me: 'Sell everything, and
give to the poor.'"

T he stories that the Desert Monastics left behind for us
to contemplate through the centuries are always a bit
provocative. They take the world as we know it and
turn it around. All of them make us rethink everything we've ever
thought about the spiritual life and make us see it differently,
newly. But this story is not just provocative. It approaches the
blasphemous. If the brother gives away the very scripture that
guides him, what kind of spiritual narcissism is that? Is he saying
that he doesn't need to follow the Scriptures anymore? That he
can be his own guide, the blind leading the blind? Is this holiness?

And what kind of a spiritual model is that for the rest of us? Is
this story a license to forget about the Scriptures just when we had
really begun to take them seriously? Shall we now forget that they
are meant to be a blueprint for life? Not simply a collection of

little isolated stories, foreign to our culture in large part, obscure in phrase and meaning as well?

Abba Evagrius speaks out of a very deep spiritual well in this story. It takes a lot of wrestling with this Word to understand it. He makes two points, not one. And then he leaves us with an unsaid third Word to discover for the rest of our lives.

His first Word is a clear one. Brother Serapion owned only one thing—his Bible. Which, incidentally, was not unusual for Desert Monastics who lived wrapped in rough cloths, wore homemade sandals, slept on the ground, and had few, if any, books besides the Scriptures. But the one thing he had, he gave away. And that thing was the very foundation of his spiritual life.

Here in this simple story we are confronted in the starkest terms with what centuries later is still a very modern attachment. Private ownership, the tendency to amass wealth, is in our time the very foundation of globalism, the sure sign of social success, and the system on which all private security depends in a capitalist world.

The glaring spiritual question of the time, then, that Evagrius and Serapion raise is, What is it that we would give away? How much of ourselves would we actually relinquish if we really believed that reducing our own consumption would leave more for the rest of the world? Or, better yet, What is it that we would not give away no matter who needed it? Our nice bed, perhaps? Our computer? Our flat-screen TV? Our second car? And in each case we must ask ourselves, Why not? What is the thread of it that holds us down like the ropes on a hot air balloon? Whatever it is that we would not give away can tell us a great deal about ourselves. These challenges are spiritually significant ones in a period when all wealth is shifting to the top and what were once the bargaining rights of the working class are fast being dismantled.

There is a second Word embedded in this text that is equally disturbing.

Serapion, Evagrius tells us, even gives away "the Book that told him to give everything away." Serapion refuses to make an idol out of anything, even religion. Religion, which is to lead us to God, often makes a god of itself. Then what? When religion itself needs to change, then we discover what is really our God: the End to which all religion is meant to point, or is it the protocols and trappings, authority structures and old canons, music and instruments, holy pictures and statues, to which we have become accustomed? It is a question that burrows deep into the soul. This Brother Serapion is an irritating fellow.

But there is a third spiritual tsunami lurking under the simplicity of this story as well. Is it possible that Serapion knows that if he keeps the first Word and sells everything he has and gives it to feed the poor, that he will have fulfilled the whole Gospel and so will not need the book anymore?

Chapter Five

HUMILITY AND LEARNING

One day Abba Arsenius was asking an old Egyptian man for advice about what he was thinking. There was someone who saw this and said to him: "Abba Arsenius, why is a person like you, who has such a great knowledge of Greek and Latin, asking a peasant like this about your thoughts?" He replied: "Indeed, I have learned the knowledge of Latin and Greek, yet I have not learned even the alphabet of this peasant."

A ny time we separate ourselves from the world around us, we lose a part of the vision it takes to become what we are meant to be—the part that cannot be developed by praying at an internal shrine to the self. The fact is, as the poet John Donne said so well, "No man is an island." None of us is sufficient unto ourselves. None of us. Not I, not you, not even presidents and popes. To learn that would be enough to make the spiritual life itself its own kind of purifying asceticism.

What the Desert Monastics knew in a very special spiritual way, long before modern psychology began to offer leadership workshops, is that when we try to function as if we are an island—distinct, invincible, detached from all others—is exactly when we fail most.

Parents who won't listen to their children, teachers who won't learn from their students, even ministers of the faith who pay no attention to the concerns and insights of those they serve, live on a very short lifeline. They are doomed to failure no matter how brilliant their first successes. It's when the doors of the inner sanctum close, when those who purport to lead close themselves off from the wisdom of the rest of the world, that nations fall and churches begin to crumble, families dissolve and friends disappear. Then, Abba Arsenius becomes a very modern figure, a spiritual man in public demand.

Arsenius comes to draw our attention to three dimensions of life—very much like the blind men in the Hindu story who circling an elephant can only define the part of it which they themselves have experienced —-the tail, the trunk, or the massive sides. Arsenius alerts us to how badly the concept of humility has deteriorated in the West—and to its peril. He requires us to examine our own abilities. He prods us to reach out and learn from the strangers among us.

In the West, where "rugged individualism" settled a pioneer continent at the expense of those people who had lived here before us, independence, initiative and personal inclinations have become national virtues. It is a matter of, "Do what you want, take what you can, resist whom you must. But get what's in front of you and get it for yourself." No more pagan a mentality than this one has ever been absorbed by Christianity since the fall of the Roman Empire.

And when the great Abba Arsenius, a Roman by birth, a leader of the monastic disciples in Scetis, reaches out to an Egyptian peasant for information, the idol falls. Arsenius knows himself to be a scholar of the classics, the most educated of ancient people. In his social circle there is nothing he doesn't know. But he also realizes that each of us is the Oracle of Delphi in some field but not in all. He does not disparage his own abilities. Humility, he knows, is no synonym for humiliation.

Instead, Arsenius has not lowered himself; he has simply put the peasant on the pedestal such a peasant deserves in the areas of his own expertise—agriculture, perhaps; the weather, perhaps; fishing, perhaps; boatbuilding, perhaps; local history or geography or social systems, perhaps. All of them worthy and noble and necessary dimensions of life. Arsenius' strength lies in knowing that his own wisdom has its limits, its boundaries.

Then comes the spiritual lesson for our own era which is at least as fraught with class tension and racial prejudice as his own. Arsenius reaches out to the stranger to fill up what is wanting in himself. And in doing that, he brings us face-to-face with ourselves and our own times. He requires us to examine how we treat foreigners. How we treat immigrants. How we regard the "other." As Jesus did the Canaanite woman, the Samaritan woman, the Roman soldier? Or the way the Romans did? Exacting from them both heavy labor and heavy taxes?

Indeed, these monastics of the desert might well be judges of our own time. They might well make us look at what it means to be a Christian in a world where we have the churches but may be on the verge of losing the charism.

Chapter Six

STUMBLING TOWARD PERFECTION

Once a brother committed a sin in Scetis, and the elders
assembled and sent for Abba Moses. He, however, did
not want to go. Then the priest sent a message to him,
saying: "Come, everybody is waiting for you." So he finally got up to go. And he took a worn-out basket with
holes, filled it with sand, and carried it along. The people who came to meet him said: "What is this, Father?"
Then the old man said: "My sins are running out behind
me, yet I do not see them. And today I have come to
judge the sins of someone else." When they heard this,
they said nothing to the brother, and pardoned him.

I t is so easy to reduce religion to do's and don'ts. But
once we start down that path, we lose touch with the
real mystery of God among us. This little monastic
story exposes the difference between the priestly dimension of
the Church and its mystical tradition.

Ecclesiastical legalism may set the standards that define the
Christian community, but Christian mysticism shows us the
effort it takes to put on the mind of Christ. It is a reminder that
there are times when we must choose between the dictates of the

institution and the beauty of the faith. It is a choice between the mission of the clerical establishment to maintain the tradition, and the deep spiritual insights of those wisdom figures who make the living tradition real. Their very lives point to what it means to see the world as God sees the world.

The universal basis of the story is a clear one: It is not about perfection. On the contrary, it is a reminder that sin we have always with us. It is an admonition to us to realize that it is the very nature of humanity to grow into God, one mistake at a time. Perfection is not what being human is about. Perfection is simply not attainable in the human condition. The function of being human is to become the best human beings we can be, one insight, one mistake, at a time. Then, knowing the struggle that comes with trying and failing over and over again, we become tender with others who are also struggling in the process.

No, if you're human and you know it, perfection is at best a mirage, and at its worst a temptation to arrogance of the highest degree. It's the temptation to make "sinners"—meaning those not us—the outcasts of the time. It separates the holy from the unholy ones. It makes clear who of us are close to God and who are not. Those who keep their Lenten resolutions we call pious. Those who always go along in silence we call humble. Those who never raise questions, especially in the Church, we call obedient. Those who attend all the rituals, we call holy. To all the others, though, such a Church as this would deny communion for seeking pluralistic ways to deal with pluralistic issues. Without even the grace to blush, this Church condemns as public sinners those who believe in equality, or conscience, or change.

But this is not the Church that teaches what Jesus taught. And this is not the Church whose teachings people recognize for their openhearted approach to the human condition. And this is not the Church each one of us knows ourselves to need.

Inside each of us, a truth rises to be heard: It is only mercy and meaning that can really deal with sin. It is the mercy we seek within ourselves that we must offer to others. It is the meaning of Jesus' presence among us that we must seek now ourselves to be.

Enter Abba Moses. Called by the priests to pass judgment on a brother, to publicly condemn the one already humiliated, Moses refuses to be part of the scene. Required by the institution to appear and do his duty, he comes but not to be part of the gaggle of those who prefer church tribunals to church teaching. Moses comes to be the presence of the healing and merciful Jesus. He at the same time comes to raise the souls of those deadened by the lashes of the law to the love of a forgiving God.

Moses condemns, yes, but not the one they expect. Moses condemns the condemners. Moses is the truly holy person, of all the church people assembled, who refuses to cast the first stone. And after all, doesn't Moses also come to condemn us all for pretending to ourselves that the law can ever satisfy for the love of God? This love, this same church teaches us, we must each pour out upon the heads of the dishonored and distressed in our own lives.

Moses comes to tell us that love without measure, love without cost, love without judgment is, after all, what all other spiritual practices are meant to develop in us.

Chapter Seven

In Search of Spiritual Depth

Amma Syncletica said: "In the beginning, there is struggle and a lot of work for those who come near to God. But after that, there is indescribable joy. It is just like building a fire: at first it's smoky and your eyes water, but later you get the desired result. Thus we ought to light the divine fire in ourselves with tears and effort."

T here are two things we need to realize when we read the sayings of the Ammas and the Abbas of desert monastics. The first important piece of information is that you don't get to be an Amma of the desert just by going there. Syncletica and her sister both devoted themselves to the spiritual life after their parents died. What they inherited they sold and gave to the poor in order to live sparse and eremitical lives. But, notice: Syncletica became an Amma, not her sister.

The second insight may be even more important than the first: To become an Amma you don't even have to go to a desert. Most of those in the early Church who really set out to concentrate only on God in their lives—thousands and thousands of them— did, in fact, move to the desert. Distractions were few there and asceticism was of the very nature of the place, but not all who lived a monastic life went to the desert. Syncletica and her sister, in fact, lived in a cave in the area of the city of Alexandria where they had grown up and lived all their lives. Obviously, being an Amma of the Desert is more a quality of soul and style of life than it is a mere fact of geography.

It also has something to do with age—with having lived long enough to have arm-wrestled the demons of life yourself before you preach too much to others. Syncletica, they say, was eighty-four when she left union with God in this world for union with the God of the universe in the next.

Ammas and Abbas, in other words, are people we can trust with our own souls because they have already been where we are going and have done it well. Having mastered their own lives, they are spiritual masters whose truths we can trust as we find ourselves embroiled in our own.

This is the Syncletica who talks to us here. Her words are precious and profound. She says to us: Don't give up. The way to God, the road to spiritual depth, is slow but true. It demands constant attention but it is worth it. In the end it brings peace and joy.

If we go through life giving away personal things to those who need them more than we do, we will find out that we did not really need them at all. The distractions we refused along the way— drinking, consumerism, excess of every possible addiction—leave us clearheaded and serene when we need it most.

The peace we were tempted to squander in life on internal wars, jealous competitions, destructive narcissism, egregious greed and spiritual emptiness, will come in a rush, Syncletica implies. Once we develop the depth it takes to turn every moment of life into the awareness of what God demands of us now, we will become the peace we seek. And we know she's right: A good marriage comes like that, a serious education comes like that, a loving relationship comes like that, and immersion in the Spirit comes like that, as well.

Start, she says. Start now. Start at this moment of life, start at whatever stage you find yourself. Choose first things first, always. Make room for reflection. Live in the Scriptures. Begin the way you want it all to end. And then it shall be so.

Chapter Eight

COMPANIONS ON THE WAY

A brother questioned Abba Hierax saying, "Give me a
Word. How can I be saved?" the old man said to him,
"Sit in your cell and if you are hungry eat; if you are
thirsty, drink; only do not speak evil of anyone, and you
will be saved."

T
he pursuit of the spiritual life is not something that is a
solitary project, even when we attempt to do it alone.
To have ourselves for a spiritual guide promises little
more for the future than the etcetera of the present. At the same
time, the constant reworking of the more-of-the-same of our lives
only deepens the darkness within us. The questions and conclu-
sions which repeat themselves in us tire us out and wear us down.
We become convinced that there is no new future possible for us,
that we are trapped in the prisons we have made for ourselves.
And, finally, aloneness only drives us to chew over, like cows revis-
iting the cud, the unfinished dimensions of our lives. The anger
we have not articulated. The resentments we have not purged.
The jealousies that yet lie within us, like sandpaper in our souls.

In the midst of our own darkness, it is not more repetition that
we need. It is fresh, new, profound light that is lacking. Which

we ourselves do not have to offer. All our private ruminations on them do nothing to resolve them because we have nothing new to bring to their analysis. By going over and over the old territory ourselves, the best we can do as we attempt to understand our own situation is rearrange the furniture of our souls. So we look at all the old questions again, from one angle or another, but see nothing new. Do nothing new. And so, no surprise: nothing ever really changes.

Because we have nothing new to bring to the situation, we are unable to move ourselves beyond the quicksand in which we stand. It's one more reprise of where we've been, perhaps, but it's not a new direction or a new way of being. It is a labyrinth without an exit. Or, as Jeremiah implies (Jeremiah 10:23) and the proverbs say, "To have oneself for a director is to have a fool for a guide."

No; to move beyond where we are in our rigid attitudes, our narrow perspectives on life, takes a fresh view of the spiritual terrain we've already traveled. The soul needs a guide to navigate these deep waters. A good friend, a spiritual model, a holy person—all bring another way of looking at what we take for granted but cannot really unravel for ourselves. The spiritual guide brings a microscope to examine both the possibilities and the obstacles we're facing in life but may not recognize. They are not mirrors meant to reflect one more eternal time what we ourselves already know about who we are and what we really seek. At this point in life, we all need someone else to help us see what we've been looking at for ages but did not ever see clearly at all.

None of these insights are new. They all belong to what it means to be human. All of us know the truth of them intuitively, if nothing else. As has everyone in every age before us.

Both the Desert Monastics in the fourth century and spiritual leaders in our own, by dint of immersion in the spiritual life themselves, know its labors. Know its pitfalls. Know its disappointments. Know its obstacles. Know the pain of wanting to be more than we believe ourselves to be. It is this inching toward God that this story of the Desert Monastics is really dealing with. More than that, it is about not getting fooled along the way.

The Word the seeker asks for is a simple one: How can I be saved? And the answer is even simpler but often overlooked. The answer has two parts. The first part of the answer is deceptively direct. It is: "Do what you do. Go about your life well." You can hear the thunderous silence of it, see the narrowing eyes of the seeker, watch the soul struggling with the implications. The simplicity of the response astounds. "Is that all?" we ask. "Is there nothing difficult to this? No drama necessary? No extreme fast? No withdrawal from people? No sacrifice of love or happiness or personal security? Then what is it all about? I do all of that already!"

The Holy One is clear: That is not what salvation, union with God, and holiness are all about. Salvation, Abba Hierax tells us, requires only that we do not speak evil of anyone. It requires us to live in peace, and to live in trust of the whole rest of the world.

Which is where the second part of the answer becomes life-changing: We are not, we are being told, to put ourselves in the place of God. We are not to write some people in but everyone else out of love of God or out of our own lives. We are not to judge the other. We are not to slander the other. We are not to discount the other. We are not to make ourselves the standard of decency or justice or religion itself.

For this kind of Holy Wisdom we need the counsel of the wise and experienced other.

Those who have already gone the way of God before us have the experience to see where we have gone astray in the spiritual life. They know the well-worn paths to God because they have spent their lives choosing one from the other. They are guides who, if we allow them, can help to save us from ourselves. They tolerate no foolish posturing in the name of sanctity. Instead they point us to the taming of the passions that hide us from ourselves. They save us from having a fool for a guide.

Chapter Nine

Hurry to Your Cell

Abba Anthony teaches, "Just as fish die if they stay too long out of water, so the monks who loiter outside their cells or pass their time with those of the world lose the intensity of inner peace. So, like a fish going toward the sea, we must hurry to reach our cell, for fear that if we delay outside we shall lose our interior watchfulness."

I n contemporary society the word "cell" is associated only with prisoners. It carries connotations of punishment and captivity. It speaks of force and control, of limitations and slavery. It stirs up the negative in us like little else. But the monk's cell is not a place of captivity; it is a place of freedom.

Monastic spirituality does not require withdrawal from the rest of humankind, but it does require interiority. In the desert, each monastic had a separate living space commonly called a cell. It was a small area in which the monk spent hours reading, praying, studying, thinking, or sleeping. To this day, monastic communities still provide small, individual rooms where the monastic can go to be alone, away from the common areas of community dinners, prayer, and work. It is where the monastic, even in a large community, can go to be silent and undisturbed. The cell is where the one immersed in thoughts of God and life can go to be alone, to seek the enlightenment the moment or task demands. This is where the monastic goes to sink into the self to think things through, to sort things out, to find the God of the Present Moment.

The cell is a precious place in the monastic life, the place where the soul flies free. Like the fish Abba Anthony speaks of in this saying, it is the monastic cell that anchors the soul in place. The problem, the Desert Monastics would say, is that everyone needs one of these. Everyone. Those who came out to the desert to seek spiritual direction were given sound spiritual advice. The Desert Monastics were not telling people how to be monks. They were telling people from all walks of life—clerical and lay—how to live the spiritual life.

Clearly one of the pillars of the spiritual life, as far as the Desert Monastics were concerned, was a time and place for reflection. A cell. A place to which we can retire in order to find our way back to our best ideals, our fullest selves, our life with God. A physical place, not a mental one, where we are truly alone and truly in peace. The cell is the place where clamor and chaos stop at the door. It's the place where we get back in touch with our best selves. It's the center of our very own, private, spiritual universe.

The great spiritual problem of the day, then, is being "like fish out of water." A life without spiritual regularity drifts through time with little to really hang onto when life most needs an anchor. Instead, we often get caught up in someone else's agenda most of our lives. We put the cell aside for work and its never-ending deadlines. We forget the cell when we need it most and make play a poor substitute for thought and prayer. We think that we can run our legs off doing, going, finding, socializing, and still stay stolid and serene in the midst of the pressure of it all. And then we find ourselves staring at the ceiling one night and thinking to ourselves, "There must be more to life than this."

The fact is that human beings need spiritual rest as well as physical rest. Psychologists deal daily with the effects on clients of stress and pressure, of frenzied work and frantic schedules, of open-plan offices and crammed buses, of swarming trains, planes, and automobiles. They see the weary and the worried, the angry and the anxious, and all of them say the same thing: I need time for myself. I need to be able to think for a while. I just need some-place quiet. We find ourselves struggling between having no job, losing a job, trying to find a job, and being smothered by the job we have. Our bills pile up and our energy goes down just trying to meet them.

It is precisely then, when life is at its most frantic, most fright-ening, that we each need a place to go to, a place that wraps us around in silence and calm. No matter who we are or what we do, we need someplace without clutter and disorganization written all over it. We need a cave that is ours. We need someplace we have put aside, a small, simple place we have designated as our doorway to peace, where we can sink into ourselves and find the God who awaits us there.

The warning from Abba Anthony is clear: We must hurry to reach our cell for fear that if we delay outside we shall lose our interior watchfulness. If we do not do this, if we stay out of our cells, out of our selves too long, we will lose our way. We will wander in the doldrums of distraction. Too far distant from quiet and calm, we will forget what it means to open the soul to the God who is always there.

Chapter Ten

CULTIVATING A CONTEMPLATIVE CONSCIOUSNESS

Amma Syncletica said, "There are many who live in the mountains and behave as if they were in town, and they are wasting their time. It is possible to be a solitary in one's mind while living in a crowd, and it is possible for one who is a solitary to live in the crowd of his own thoughts."

I t is true that monastic spirituality clings to the notion of the cell as the place of quiet and inner peace, of contemplation and union with God. But it is also true that the physical space itself, as important as it is, very easily can be confused with the real thing. All the cells in the world will not save us from our own lack of mental discipline and contemplative consciousness.

Religious language itself commonly misuses the two realities. We use "cloister" and "contemplative" as if they were synonyms. We assume that cloister—the physical withdrawal from interaction with others—will of itself make contemplatives of us. In that case, the Jesus who walked from Galilee to Jerusalem, crushed by the crowds, thronged by the sick, hounded by authorities, and entreated on every side, could not have been a contemplative. Or to put it another way, the One who said, "The Father and I are One," when the specification of space becomes an essential element of contemplation, does not qualify. Nothing in the history of spirituality confirms that position. Mystics for centuries have described life in the consciousness of the presence of God as the unitive state of the spiritual life.

But more than anybody's definition, history is clear proof that some of our most active saints have been deeply contemplative. It was, in fact, precisely the deeply contemplative awareness of God's will for the world that drove them to activities that changed the world around them. Catherine of Siena, Teresa of Avila, Benedict of Nursia, Ignatius of Loyola, Hildegard of Bingen, Francis of Assisi, and multiple others immersed themselves in the Word of God and followed it.

Indeed, Amma Syncletica is clear: Going to the mountains— hiding away—won't make anybody a contemplative. And living in the city won't obstruct it either.

The truth is that it is where the mind is that determines where the heart beats, where the soul thrives. It is what nourishes us that grows us beyond the mundane and sends us into the heart of God. It is in our minds that the point of Oneness exists. "It is possible to be a solitary in one's mind while living in a crowd," Amma Syncletica teaches the seeker. But just as important to understand when we undertake the search for God within us, "It is possible for one who is a solitary to live in the crowd of his own thoughts." We can, that is, drown out the presence of God in us by using separation from others to concentrate only on ourselves.

The point is clear: What we bring to the pursuit of the God of life is what we will get out of it. The regularity of prayer, the depth of our lectio, the embrace of silence, the space we give to the search for God, the surrender of our own obsessions with self to the concerns of God for the world—all these will determine the quality of the contemplation we achieve.

Prayer becomes the olive press we walk, the chafing wheel we tread which, over and over again, breaks open our hearts to the Word of God. Then, finally, after years of immersion in daily prayer, we begin to be what we have prayed for all those years.

Lectio, sacred reading, the time we spend wrestling with the Word of God, determines the degree of understanding we bring to the life we live, wherever we live it. Contemplative silence is more than not speaking. It is the ability to find the center of the self and give it over to the presence of God. Real silence wipes clean the clutter of the soul. It puts down the clamor that claims our soul and puts openness to God in its place.

The amount of time we give to all of these bits and pieces of the Holy Quest makes the difference between seeking God and dabbling in the spiritual life. Then, possessed by the Presence of God, we do not quibble about the definitions of the contemplative life anymore. The God within becomes the rudder, the mast and the compass of life for us. Then, we live in God as well as having God live in us.

At that point, Amma Syncletica's words do not confuse us anymore. They free us to be with God wherever we are because God—finally, finally, finally, as we now know—God is indeed everywhere.

Chapter Eleven

GOD'S AGENTS ON EARTH

One day Abba Daniel and Abba Ammoes went on a journey together. Abba Ammoes said, "When shall we, too, settle down in a cell, Father?" Abba Daniel replied, "Who shall separate us henceforth from God? God is in the cell, and, on the other hand, He is outside, too."

A bba Daniel's story is a particularly interesting one. It shrinks the space between the fourth century Desert Monastics and the spiritual seekers of the twenty-first century down to nothing. Not much has really changed it seems. Lest we are inclined to think that monastics of the desert in the fourth century had one common view of life, it's time to think again. Abba Daniel and Abba Ammoes, the younger monk, are both of them in an Egyptian desert in a period of great change in society. They see life through two different filters.

Abba Daniel, the elder, the spiritual father or guide of the younger man, knows that life is a whole. He has been in the desert for years. He knows by now that monastic life in the desert is no more protective of the spiritual life than it would be anywhere else.

Abba Ammoes, on the other hand, sees the world—life outside his cell—as his spiritual enemy. He wants to know when they will be safely back in their cells again, spiritual again, religious again. He's young and likes rules and social norms by which to measure himself.

We do very much the same in our own time, it seems. We compartmentalize life between the sacred and the secular. Religion on Sundays: work and play all the other days of the week. Care for the poor when we make out our taxes: profit-making every other day of the week. In theocratic societies, societies in which State and Church are one, it seems to work. The public schedule is a spiritual one. Feast days and feria days—religious festivals and events outside the religious calendar—are the same for everyone. Religion is part of the public structures. But in a pluralistic world—a world where no single religion has public preeminence—religion tends to become a private thing. People schedule it and practice it and celebrate it as they see fit, often alone, always separately from everyone else.

But Abba Daniel is truly religious, truly immersed in God, truly contemplative. He sees everything in life as the Word of God, teaching him something, requiring something from him in return. "What can separate us from God?" he asks the young man. Meaning, of course, except ourselves. He does not claim for himself either difference or privilege. He moves into his cell as the same person who came out of it. The same values, the same obligations, the same goals. Like Jesus, he moves into and out of his cell freely, he moves easily with the world around him. Like

Jesus, he is in the world but not of it. He does not lose himself in its values when he is outside his cell.

Abba Daniel, wise old monk, knows that the purpose of the spiritual life is not to separate us from others. On the contrary, it is meant to unite us, but all too often it is used to divide us. Only the really spiritual, the real religious in every tradition, know that the One God wants us all to be one. We are meant to identify with the hopes and fears, and the needs and struggles, of the whole world—because the world is God's, and we are God's agents on earth. No, the world cannot separate us from God. Only we can do that.

The Desert Fathers, steeped in the Scriptures and in the mind of God, were of one mind about where God is. God is everywhere. It all depends on where we are. Hiding somewhere afraid of losing God in God's world, we lose the Words of God the world has to say to us.

We know this is true because we have seen how those who believe that God is only in churches, not in the world, have no compunction about destroying the world. They have no fear of clogging its rivers, polluting its skies, slaughtering its animals, and clearing its forests. They do not worry about God's future; they care only for their own "cell," their own time, their own tomorrow. It is a pallid and bare kind of spirituality. It makes religion a creature's paradise but not a creature's responsibility.

Those who like Ammoes want the comfort of their place in the universe must hear the word from Daniel. To recognize our responsibility to be its keepers. Otherwise, what do we really know about the presence of God?

Chapter Twelve

THE NARROW GATE

Amma Theodora said, "Let us strive to enter by the narrow gate. Just as the trees, if they haven't stood before the winter's storms cannot bear fruit, so it is with us; this present age is a storm and it is only through many trials and temptation that we can obtain an inheritance in the kingdom of heaven."

A mma Theodora is a woman for our own times. She knows that no religious regimen alone can possibly make us truly spiritual people. She knows that it is not what we do to satisfy our religious obligations that makes us holy. It is, instead, what we do when it seems impossible to do anything to make the world the place God means it to be. It is making the world in any way religious at all that tests the mettle in us. Then we can see the effect of the religious practices we do. Then we come to know what it means to "enter through the narrow gate."

"This age is a storm," she says, "and it is only through many trials" that we can build the Kingdom of Heaven in times such as this. It is character, she tells us, it is the quality of goodness in a person, that is truly spiritual and that is demanded in difficult times.

The word of the Desert Ammas to our own age is a serious one: To be truly spiritual people in our own time, rote religion will not do. Only by applying the Word of God to the issues of the day can we ever hope to claim to be disciples now. The issues we face now confront every value the Gospel preaches. Immigration, poverty and equality test the very reality of discipleship. How do we practice hospitality in a global world where the destitute refugee has followed the cash crops taken from her own country to the garbage cans of this one? How can we call ourselves caring and saying nothing about the care of refugees? What do we do to alleviate poverty when money rushes to the top of the economic ladder while food stamps for the poor are reduced? How do we call ourselves Christian and say nothing about massive economic imbalance? On what Christian values do we stand when we deny half the population of the world—women—equal wages, equal political representation, and freedom from rape and domestic violence?

To read Amma Theodora and shrug off the responsibility is impossible. Virtue, she says, requires the test of Christian values. And those who do not stand up for them, do not have them.

Yes, storms strengthen, she concedes, but they also prune. They sweep away dead wood and weak roots. They leave standing as live and fruit-bearing trees only those who have withstood the raging hurricane of evil that Christians face in times like these. When the poor, the displaced, and women are simply dismissed rather than liberated and Christians have nothing to say about that, the Gospel is not being preached. When Christian do nothing to change these things, their religion is pure show.

The picture with which Amma Theodora confronts us is a picture of resistance in the face of great blustering power. "Stand up!" she says. Do the really valiant work of Christianity. Say no to oppression, and say yes to justice and always to equality. Do not seek the easy way of conformity to social power. Defy the powerful who smother the small. Go through the narrow gate, the gate of struggle with those who struggle. Go through the narrow gate of refusal to collude with domination. Support those who buck the tide of prejudice and reject the notion of natural inferiority. In other words, Go the way of Jesus. Don't just read the Gospel, require that where you are, steps are taken to bring it. For all our sakes.

Most interesting of all about this story, perhaps, is that Amma Theodora does not promise victory or immediate success or even much in the way of public support. She talks about next year's fruit, still growing on the newly strengthened trees that made it through the storm. She talks about understanding that each of us is just one more step to the fullness of the Kingdom of God. We may not see the victory, she implies, but that is irrelevant. What counts is simply that we be part of enabling it to come.

There is another story on this subject that Amma Theodora did not know but I think would have loved if only she had heard it. It's from the Scripture of Nature:

"How many snowflakes does it take to break a branch?" the old owl asked the snowflake.

"I don't have a clue," the little snowflake replied.

"Then, if you don't know if you can do it, why do you continue?" the owl pressed.

"Because," the little snowflake said, "I want to do my part."

We all have a part in the changing of the world. It will go the way we go. The great spiritual problem lies in understanding that. Then, like the snowflake, we must spend our lives to do our part in changing it from the mundane into the Kingdom of God.

Chapter Thirteen

LOVE WILL PREVAIL

Abba Pambo said, "If you have a heart, you can be saved."

T he stark simplicity of this Word from a desert eighteen centuries before us is itself a message. Surely a statement such as this cannot be correct. Not in a society that thrives more on what it *has* than what it *is* at any given global moment.

After all, one thing we know in the West: No matter what we do for which others may exact revenge, we can save ourselves. No matter what we fail to do for which others require compensation, we can save ourselves. Neither revenge nor compensation worry us. After all, what we have is power. Force. Weaponry unheard of, unimagined, by any other people on the globe. We can exterminate whole societies, their women and children with them. We can pulverize our enemies into oblivion. We can withstand the scorn, the disdain, the disgust of the entire world.

And until we do it, we will have no idea how we will be destroying ourselves at the same time. All of our relationships with the rest of the human race will have been destroyed. All of the gifts that come from the gifts of other cultures around us in the world will be suspended. All of the sense of being human with humans everywhere will have been forfeited. Everything for which we need the services of the rest of the world will go up in the flames we have set. And we will survive to live in the new Dark Ages we have created. And so, we will not really survive at all.

No, weapons will not save us. Force is not our answer. Power is powerless to resolve anything by force because eventually it will consume itself. Like Sparta, when everything goes into the military, everything else eventually deteriorates: the infrastructure of a country, the social services of a people, the educational system that makes a nation a dynamic force in the world community and, most of all, the sense of moral purpose, global justice, and social equality that makes a nation strong.

On what can we possibly root our hope then? What will save us when we have nothing left but power with which to make our way through the community of life? From whom may we expect compassion if we ourselves have no history of forgiveness? From where can we hope for understanding, if all we have to offer the world is retribution without end?

The only thing that can possibly save us, Abba Pambo tells us, is what we have inside ourselves. Only one dimension of life can save us from ourselves. Abba Pambo is clear: "If you have a heart, you can be saved."

To the ancient world, the human heart was more than the seat of human feelings, more than an icon of human emotion as we are most likely to regard it now. The heart, to the Desert Monastics and the culture around them, was the spiritual point of intersection that made the human, human. From the heart came the wellspring of spirit and action, insight and will, sensitivity and meaning— that brought the individual to fullness of life. To lack any of these dimensions of life was to lack what it takes to live consciously, spiritually, and lovingly.

Unbounded emotion, important as feeling is to human direction, is an insufficient approach to any issue. It connects us to the feelings of the world, an essential dimension to understanding the impact of our actions on others, but it does not resolve the situation. Understanding and emotions do not change the past or cure the present. Only conversion of the spirit can do that.

Insight into an issue may well suggest a direction out of it. But the intellectual appreciation of a problem gives us, at most, a series of options for action. Simply doing something differently does not guarantee that change of direction alone will resolve a problem. In fact, bad choices can make problems worse. World War II Germany went from democracy, to dictatorship, to militarism, to total destruction and defeat in a period of ten years. Options are clearly only part of any solution.

In the end, spirit alone determines what we have to bring to every situation. It is what we have within us that determines whether we have what it takes both to save a situation and to save ourselves.

If the spirit is good, steeped in the Word of God and livened by the mercy of it, then the situation is resolvable. Love will prevail and, at the same time, justice will be done.

If the spirit is bad, no good will come of it. Closed to the other, driven by emotions dipped in poison, bent on destruction rather than development, the situation will only deteriorate. If control rather than conversion of heart—our own as well as the other's—is its goal, that kind of spirit will only make a bad situation worse.

When the heart goes sour the human being goes astray, humanity withers before our eyes, and the salvation of our small, hurting world will need to wait for someone else. Someone, as Abba Pambo said, with heart.

Chapter Fourteen

STEEPED IN GOD'S WORD

Abba Poemen said, "The nature of water is soft, that of stone is hard; but if a bottle is hung about the stone, allowing the water to fall drop by drop, it wears away the stone. So it is with the Word of God; it is soft and our heart is hard, but the one who hears the Word of God often opens his heart to God."

T he monastics of the desert, living in harsh places under an even harsher sun, understood what it was to wrestle with the demands of the self. Their lives were not about seeking physical comfort. They did not concentrate on personal security. Public approval was not their drug of choice. No, the Desert Monastics lived to bring their souls to heel. They looked themselves in the eye and faced what they saw. If it was impatience, they set out to tame it. If it was anger that plagued them, they devoted themselves to exposing the venom within. If lassitude weighed them down, they drove themselves to even greater levels of practice, even deeper levels of prayer.

But most of all, they turned to the Scriptures for the model of life that could sustain all burdens and achieve all depths of soul. And they lived in it—night and day, day and night. But why? And how? They did it to put on the mind of God for the world. The way they did it, and the method they leave to us now, is total immersion.

The secret to the monastic study of the Scriptures is repetition to the point of total recall. It is a matter of reading the Scriptures morning, noon, and night of every day. It is the daily placing of the self in the presence of Jesus in order to become what we see.

This ongoing dialogue of the soul with the Word, from one year to the next, challenged their every thought and wish and reaction. It led them on through each phase and stage of themselves until all the juice of the Word seeped into their souls never to be forgotten. The model of the living Jesus prodded their souls from stage to stage.

When they were young, what they saw in the way Jesus contended with the religious authorities of his time was, at very least, an exercise in courage. At the same time, as the years went by, they also saw an equally strong lesson in probative but gentle disagreement. They grew from insight to insight with every presentation of the same Gospel, over and over again. They grew once, twice, and always as each new whisper of the Word reshaped them from spiritual child to spiritual visionary.

Growth, in the monastic model, is a slow process, borne out of experience and shaped by listening. First, and foremost, the Desert Monastic listened to the spiritual guide whose years in the desert were sign of perseverance in the spiritual life. The spiritual father or mother, the Abba or the Amma, were those who knew what it was to try and fail, but try again. Tested by years of fidelity to the way of life, they were living signs of the effectiveness of the desert life in shaping holy people.

People from the cities, as well as disciples who were themselves considering commitment to the life, flocked to them for spiritual direction. The Words were clearly as important to the average person as they were to those who intended to follow the eremitical life. That these Words touched people of every level of life speaks volumes about their essential value to them and to us, both then and now. The Desert Monastics were not recruiting; they were leading a whole level of society to a living spiritual well. And, it seems, they speak to us yet.

Interestingly enough, it was not their asceticism that singled the Desert Monastics out as spiritual teachers. It was the basic principles of which they spoke—the fruit of their fasting and prayer—that became their spiritual legacy. Their commitment to religious rigor and the wilderness faded in public impact as the years went by, but their teachings got more and more important. Here were people who, having lived a rugged life cut off from society at large, had words of wisdom for the larger society that little else could match. And that Word was what it meant to think as Jesus thought and to become another presence of Jesus in the world. Now. Again. Newly. Through us.

The spiritual life, they taught, was about allowing the Word of God, the life of Jesus, to seep into their souls. Those hardened by the values of the world could then be softened, day by day, by the words of Jesus. It was a matter of hearing over and over again, "And Jesus, looking at them, loved them," or Jesus saying, "Do not send them away," or Jesus directing, "The people are hungry; feed them yourselves"—and takes the clay of the human soul and softens it.

At that point, Abba Poemen knew, hardness of heart would disappear before the Word of God and the world would become new because, this time, it would be our presence that would make it so.

Chapter Fifteen

PASSIONS THAT LIE IN WAIT

Abba Zosimas said, "It was well said once by a wise person, that the soul has as many masters as it has passions. And again, the Apostle says, 'People are slaves to whatever masters them.'" (2 Peter 2:19)

I
t's difficult for the modern mind to imagine that time in an Egyptian desert could possibly be the most difficult, plaguing, uncomfortable moment of a person's spiritual life. But the Desert Monastics knew better. To go into the desert was to "do battle for Christ." It was the moment of great withdrawal from the world, but not because the world was necessarily bad. The problem lay in the fact that the noise and activity of the world had the capacity to distract seekers from the greatest problem of them all: themselves. The Desert Monastics went to the desert not to escape the sins of the world, but to confront their own.

The lesson is a crucial one for us as well as for them, for this century as well as for any century before us. The great spiritual truth is this: Inside us all is the real struggle of our lives. It's not the enemy next door that is the great spiritual nemesis of our lives; it's how we *deal* with the enemy next door that determines the quality of our own souls and the tenor of our lives. Or, to put it another way, it's not the affluence and temptations that come with money that is the problem, it's the way we deal with money that is the problem. Or the way we deal with anger. Or the way we deal with impatience, maybe.

It is, in other words, our own passions that "lie in wait" for us in the silence of our deserts. It is the allurements and excesses to which we have given over our lives that really determine its character and tone. Happiness, the Desert Monastics knew with fierce insight, does not come from outside ourselves. Happiness is the fruit of the degree of peace and contentment that we have developed within us.

The language of this monastic definition of happiness is different from ours but clear, nevertheless: Zosimas says, "The soul has as many masters as it has passions." But at his time, in this case, the word passion does not have the overtones of ardor or fervor or spirit in the sense of excitement. Passion to the Desert Monastic means "a wound of the soul"; the inclinations in us which, if not curbed, can only bring distress. These are the undertows of the human spirit which, if we give in to them, bring suffering down upon our own heads.

It is a warning echoed throughout the early history of spirituality. Julian of Norwich in her *Showings* put it best. "God does not punish sin," Julian said, "sin punishes sin." And who has struggled with their addictions, emotional or physical, and does not know the truth of it! Curing ourselves of the impulses in us that are eating us alive are so much more difficult than falling captive to them in the first place.

The Desert Fathers and Mothers did not hesitate to name what the Christian tradition would later call the Seven Capital Sins: anger, gluttony, lust, greed, envy, and, in desert language, vainglory and acedia. The warnings are as important today as they were in the deserts centuries ago.

Anger eats out our insides. It refuses to let go of old hurts and new fears until our hearts go to dust from the raging flame it lights within us.

Gluttony leads us to engorge ourselves on rich foods and fine drinks. Taste becomes the center of our lives and makes us prisoners of our bellies. Satisfaction engages us.

The lust that makes love impossible and leaves peace of soul in tatters makes any kind of spiritual contentment impossible and the gift of real love unattainable.

Greed destroys the very joy it sets out to achieve. Security is a fleeting hope if security comes to mean that we must always have more and more and more of everything.

Envy takes the joy out of living. Everybody else's life poisons ours. We believe our life not good enough, not blessed enough, not full enough, not acclaimed enough. And so we drown in our own inadequate juices.

Vainglory—boastfulness and presumption of place—dooms us to disappointment as we watch others, more accomplished and more humble, receive the applause we have reserved—no, *required*—for ourselves.

And acedia—lethargy, passivity and stagnation—smothers our souls. The natural joy and energy of life die in mid-flight. Real happiness, the happiness that comes from a sense of purpose and the fullness of God, requires more attention than we have the spiritual stamina to expend on it. We simply don't care very much about anything. We are dying in our torpor, out of touch with life, out of touch with ourselves, out of touch with God.

Then Zosimas' warning takes life here and now as well as then and there: "People are slaves to whatever masters them," he teaches us. It is surely a call to the spoiled children of the twenty-first century for whom surfeit is a natural expectation. And who, as a result, will never be surfeited. It is, if the truth is to be known, a call to free ourselves from ourselves so that we can really live.

Chapter Sixteen

CHOOSE YOUR LIFE

Abba Ammonas was asked, "What is the narrow and hard way?" (Matt. 7:14) "The narrow and hard way is this, to control your thoughts, to strip yourself of your own will for the sake of God. This is also the meaning of the sentence, 'Lo, we have left everything and followed you.'" (Matthew 19:27)

T he Desert Monastics are so delightfully direct: no jargon here, no high-sounding rhetoric, no theological clichés. Just an answer, clear and unadorned. When a seeker asks Abba Ammonas how to live the good life, the life that Jesus is talking about in the Gospel, his response is a simple one: First, it depends on what kinds of things you think about. Second, it depends on what you do. Finally, it depends on *why* you do what you do. End of discussion.

The narrow and hard way, he says, is a straight and narrow path. It does not admit of bits and pieces of commitment, of stop-and-go kinds of spirituality. It is a defined direction, not a theological discussion. It's not about speculation or theological conundrums; it's about a personal determination to live life one way rather than another. It means that we must resolve exactly what we want our lives to be like—and then we must decide what it will take to achieve that. Do we want to be honest? Do we hope to be spiritual people? Shall we sell all our goods, too, and give to the poor? And if so, What? Or will life be one hit-and-miss experience after another, sometimes good, more often mediocre?

The meaning of this Word is hard to misunderstand. It's not meant to confuse us or to mislead us or to spin us into philosophical speculation. Instead, the answer is stark and unambiguous: Life is not an accident. What happens to us happens either because we did choose it—or we did not. Either choice is, in the end, a choice. What Abba Ammonas is telling us here is that we don't stumble into life with God. We don't dabble in the good life. We need to choose it. Consciously. Surely. With determination.

In his reference to Jesus' answer to questions about the purpose of life, Abba Ammonas talks about two gates to life. Both open onto a road. The first road, marked by a large gate, is broad and undefined. Large groups of people go through that one, not sure of where it leads, not much concerned about what it will demand, but willing to go along if for no other reason than that they have to go somewhere. So why not go along with all these others who believe that a little theology is enough and too much theology is boring?

For this group, life is at most an adventure. We go through life swept one way or another by the tilt of the crowd. Where they go, we go. It's easier that way. We cover our life decisions with the adolescent argument that "everyone is doing it." And so, there-fore, must we. We go, in other words, to be part of the crowd. To be liked. To get ahead. To be a success. Or worse: to get by without having to do much. Or maybe to stand out in the crowd. Or to resist the empty flow of humanity to even emptier ends. And, if truth were told, there's nothing really wrong with going in that direction. Except mediocrity. Except allowing others to choose your life, your values, your goals for you.

For those who choose the road less traveled, though, the one that opens through the narrow gate, there is a better end in sight. There are standards that must be kept. There are great spiritual figures to follow. There are great spiritual Ammas and Abbas to learn from. There are practices that can shape your soul and sharpen your mind and soften your heart as we go.

It is not an easy way. It has a purpose. It demands preparation. It seeks one thing and one thing only: the coming of the Will of God in this world and the next.

The followers on this road do not think of success here in this life as the success they seek. They do not think of power as a reason or right to do anything. They do not seek profit alone while so many are poor. They do not satiate their senses; they nourish their souls. They live lives that have meaning for others as well as joy for themselves. They know that God alone is worth the journey. And they are happy with "enough," happy with serving, at peace with one another and full of the kind of love that makes the whole world one.

In the end, the world is changed by these few. They hold up the light for a darkened world to follow. They chant the Alleluias that remind the world what really is treasure, its end. They bring Life to life.

Chapter Seventeen

BENEFICIAL TEMPTATIONS

Abba Zosimas used to say: "Take away the thoughts and no one can become holy. One who avoids the beneficial temptations is avoiding eternal life.

"It is like I always say: Inasmuch as He is good, God has given us to profit from everything. However, we become attached and misuse God's gifts; and so we turn these very same good gifts to destruction through our evil choice and are therefore harmed."

I n Abba Zosimas' reflection on the spiritual life lies a fresh and refreshing insight. All things are from God. All things. Both good gifts and beneficial temptations. Neither of them guarantees spiritual doom. Nor does either of them guarantee wholeness. It all depends on what we do with each of them—both the gifts and the temptations—as they come.

To have the gift of silence, for instance, is no surety that what we do with the silence we crave will really benefit the growth of our souls. If we spend it in interior noise—in plots and schemes meant to make us rich or powerful, in emotional tempests and turmoil because our last schemes have been thwarted—then the silence itself becomes our problem. It is spiritual cacophony at its worst. It looks good but it's actually harmful to us because we have allowed the silence to become corroded.

Plunged into the midst of our demons—jealousy or pride, for instance—we become only more trapped in them, however secretive we are about the hold they have over us. Even now. Even here.

It is what we harbor in our souls from the past that too easily becomes the character of our souls today. Indeed, such a silence as that is not the silence that brings peace. This is not the silence that brings understanding. These are not moments of self-knowledge and renewed commitment. These are not times of resting in the arms of God. No, these are the moments we have yet to put down. Instead they go on searing our hearts and scarring our souls on the hot coals of another era. These are the moments that make us our own spiritual jailors. When we don't dispel them, they go on burning in our hearts. And we wonder why our souls wither!

The Desert Monastics called those things "demons" which were the tendencies in ourselves to corrupt the human heart, to turn the mind away from the things that matter. All that happens in situations like this is that something good—a penchant for silence—turns into a surrender to the demons within. At the same time, these holy ancestors of ours did not consider our struggles with our demons to be measures of failure. On the contrary. As Abba Zosima says, there are such things as "beneficial temptations." Out of every struggle good is meant to come, not evil.

If we do not struggle with the addictions of the soul—lust, anger, jealousy, pride, power, sloth, self-centeredness—we will never really be free. We will never know the valor of those who, having had the struggle themselves, in the end consciously chose another way.

We will never understand the depths of real humility until we have known the pitfalls of pride, the emptiness of the false self we parade before the world, untried and overblown. The self we have fabricated for ourselves, groundless and empty, has no power to save us from ourselves.

Temptation is the gift of possibility. It takes us to the crossroads of life and requires us to choose a direction rather than simply fall into one. It makes virtue—spiritual strength—a reality rather than simply a word.

Most of all, for those for whom the choice is a long and painful one—years of addiction, a lifetime full of delusions of grandeur, the continuing plague of unsatisfied lust without the calming antidote of real love—there is, at the same time, another kind of gift. It is the gift of going on.

The gift of perseverance in the journey to wholeness is the treasure trove of the human spirit. Sanctity, like everything else in life, is not an event. It is a process of coming to know the clay of the self and then shaping it into a thing of beauty. This thing called union with God, sanctity, holiness, is not a matter of going through religious hoops. It is a matter of winning the contest with the self that leads us to the best in us. Becoming holy is not an attempt to become someone else. It's about becoming the fullness of ourselves.

The contender in the contest to becoming everything we are meant to be is not God. It is not against the will of God for us that we struggle. The God who made us knows the dust from which we came and gives us a lifetime to shape it. No, as Abba Zosimas knows only too well, it is we ourselves who stand between an empty life and a life with God. When we finally give ourselves over to the life-long competition between what we want to do in life and what we want to be, then we will find that we are already in the arms of God.

Chapter Eighteen

THE SPIRITUAL VALUE OF ROUTINE

Abba Poemen said of Abba Pior that every single day he made a fresh beginning.

I n a runaway world of multiple options and the myth of limitless possibilities, this tiny insight into what it means to be fully alive is easily lost in the shuffle. Modern life has two more common dimensions to steer from: The first is to quit what does not excite us. The very thought that there might be something to learn in the monotony of "Now" that could shape our futures in far more promising ways simply eludes us. The second invitation, on the other hand, is to go tunelessly on in some kind of underwater ballet that comes from nowhere and never ends. Both of those alternatives squeeze the juices of life dry.

If newness is the elixir of life, if everything is not exciting, we want no part of it. And so we stand to miss the spiritual value of routine, of simply being able to sink into the moment without the tension that comes from having to cope with one difference after another all our days.

On the other hand, if challenge has become the signpost of our lives, what *could* happen becomes more important than what *is* happening. As a result, the tension that comes from the fear of impending doom smothers the quality of the present. It squanders what could otherwise be a good time to appreciate the present in worry about a future that has yet to come.

It is precisely here where Abba Poemen and Abba Pior, two of the early desert's most sought after spiritual guides, emerge again. As they did in ages past, their lives and wisdom which seem so other than ours, come to help us find our way through a life now filled with dread and debacle on every side. The Abbas know that life is what comes from within us, not from what clings to the cloaks of our heart, demanding our attention and draining our resources.

Into this climate of spiritual ennui, of dulling sensitivities, boredom takes over. And it is boredom that smothers the soul. Bored, we lose sight of the beautiful in our midst. Bored, we overlook the world's call for our attention. Bored, we ourselves become lethargic, out of touch, and uncaring about the needs and questions of others.

So, what is the cure for such shrinkage of soul? Abba Poeman is clear: We must forever remember, each and every day of life, to make a new beginning. It is this beginner's mind—this stage of perpetual alertness—that keeps us in tune with the songs of the rest of the world.

We cannot afford to become world's unto ourselves, then. But, oh, what a seduction it is to want to free myself from the agendas of the human race! Just think about it: No more need to keep abreast of today. Of who is doing what. Or who is calling and wants a callback. Or what might be a better way of doing what we're doing. Or who will care for families that have been moved to the streets where no address is the worst address of all. Life, we have decided, is simply a long, slow drift to eternity. And in the meantime, it is all someone else's problem.

The call from the Desert Monastics is a totally different one than the call to irresponsibility like the one we ourselves are toying with at present. It is a call to begin again, every day of our lives, to complete the work on earth that the Creator has begun for us to finish. Life is a community enterprise. What we do not do for the other, will not be done for us. Our interests affect the world. And their needs affect our own. Pathological individualism, national chauvinism, and racial superiority are the scourge of the human race. The fact is that we simply cannot exist in a world unto ourselves.

Every day, like Abba Poeman, we must begin to see again our role in the creation of the world, in the development of the human race, and in the preservation of the planet. For any of us to excuse ourselves from those obligations is like the story of Cain and Abel, and to bring ourselves before the broken heart of the God for judgment. Every day, we must begin again to see again that we are "our brother's keeper" and begin anew to make that call to co-creation real.

Chapter Nineteen

WHO IS YOUR GOD?

Abba Sisoes says: "Seek God and not where God lives."

D own deep, in the most secret part of our heart's well, something forever beckons us beyond the present, above the mundane. Whatever our life situation, it urges us to immerse ourselves in a period of reflection on the purpose of life and the significance of our own life. One thing becomes apparent quickly: Life is a journey whose endpoint is always a stretch away. The more we have, the more we grasp. And then the realization dawns: Even if we have gained every-thing worth having in life, none of those things will ever satisfy the emptiness within.

Whatever captivates us along the way—money, status, freedom, power, even the spiritual life—in the end, delude us. None of them will last. None of them guarantee total satisfaction. However in command of all the trinkets of life we may be, there is yet a taste for something else. Then we come to understand that what we seek cannot be packaged and saved. Life turns and twists, brims with life and then dies a withering death, fills us up and lets us down again until, finally, we learn to seek what is but cannot be grasped.

Even religion, Abba Sisoes warns the disciples, often comes in camouflage. The thousands of disciples who flocked to the desert to learn from the Desert Monastics how to be holy, how to live a better life, found there little comfort in religious formula. The Desert Monastics were not selling amulets or prayer forms, secret devotions or life-changing asceticisms. They do not send us to the latest spiritual guru. They do not sell us the most recent mantra. They look only at our own personal commitment to finding the God of Life. The Desert Monastics taught only what it meant to live in the presence of God.

Religious practices are meant to be guides to the living God, the One who lives in us and breathes in us and walks through life with us however barren the journey may be. But they are not to be ends in themselves. Consciousness of the presence of God and practices designed to create consciousness are two different things. The problem, Abba Sisoes knew, is that it is easy to confuse the two.

Ceaselessly repeating a spiritual practice is no warrant whatsoever to believe that the repetition itself binds us to the mind of God in life. On the contrary. Spiritual practices are meant merely to remind us of the presence of God in the moment. It is when we grow beyond the pain of the moment to an understanding of what the moment brings to our own spiritual growth that we become truly spiritual people.

It is one thing to make a pilgrimage to the desert to find God. It is entirely another to be open to finding God where we are.

Then we become what the challenge of the moment summons us to be. Then Abba Sisoes' word of spiritual advice—to seek God and not simply the trappings of the spiritual life—becomes real, becomes true.

Life is not an exercise in spiritual gymnastics. It is one long, unending attempt to put on the mind of God wherever we are, whatever happens to us on the way. We are not here to pray our way out of life's challenges. We are here to grow though every one of them into spiritual adulthood. With God at our side and on our mind and in our heart, our own spiritual strength and insight grow to full stature. The transformation from body to spirit is then complete: Physically we accept the growth that takes us beyond physicality. Being the strongest, the fittest, even the most religious doesn't count anymore. Only the development of soulfulness counts now.

The souls that are totally immersed in the consciousness of God see things differently. The calendar of life—childhood, early adulthood, maturity, freedom—they know as only one of multiple stages of life. Each of the many stages of life, they come to understand, are gifts to be treasured and years to be shaped. With each of them comes new awareness that life is about growing into God, one season at a time. To try to capture any of these moments forever, to attempt to shape any of them to my own eternal ends, is to live life without coming to understand it. To seek to cement the fountain of youth or to wrest to our own insights the eternal apex of power, to cling to any single period and call it life, is to have missed the God of Life entirely.

Abba Sisoes demands an answer from each of us: Who is your God? A cornucopia of good things for spiritual children or a co-creator of life who waits for us to see the world as God sees the world and then do our part to make all of it holy? It is Emmanuel, God-with-us, that we seek. The shrines and special prayers and holy pilgrimages along the way are spiritual oases meant to build our strength for the rest of the way. They are not God; they are simply signs that the God who made us is with us. It is that relationship that counts far beyond any particular devotion.

Abba Sisoes held the secret of the really spiritual life. However faithfully we have cultivated a favorite devotion, he warns us, we are not to allow ourselves to be beguiled by any of them. Each and all of them have only one purpose. They are meant simply to point in the direction of the consciousness of God at all times and in all places.

Chapter Twenty

BE STILL AND KNOW GOD

One of the fathers said: "Just as it is impossible to see your face in troubled water, so also the soul, unless it is clear of alien thoughts, is not able to pray to God in contemplation."

J ust as we go from one event to another, looking for the answers to our questions, wanting more comfort than change, seekers flocked to the desert to learn from the Desert Monastics there. They wanted to know how to pray, how to live closer to God in time while they continued to be responsible for the secular edges of life as well as dedicated to the sacred ones. And they wanted short cuts to all of them—just as we do. Like us, too, they never failed to be surprised at the word of instruction they received there. No great sacrifices were ever expected. No complex rituals were ever required. The monastic answer to the disciples, it seems, always dealt with learning to live well where they were, rather than trying to escape from their life of daily responsibilities.

In today's case, the answer is a particularly blunt one. "Unless the soul is clear of alien thoughts, it is impossible to pray to God in contemplation." The Word is unadorned in its definition, clear in its meaning. God is not hiding from us, the words imply. We are hiding from God. Noise, the monastics teach us, is the barrier we put between ourselves and the contemplation of God with us.

Today's instruction, in fact, is all about noise. Noise, the holy one teaches, is what separates us even from ourselves. But if the people of third-century Egypt had a problem, what can possibly be said of our own generation? We even have a problem because the culture of birdsong, the culture of rural quiet, has become the culture of cacophony. Twenty-four hours a day our world crackles with Rock and Rap and Country and Beat and idle talk and senseless complaint. It's these words that do our thinking for us. Twenty-four hours a day this kind of noise substitutes for what might have become our own insights. Their meaningless presence everywhere—in stores, and offices, on street corners and in cars—distorts our search for the contemplative awareness of God in life. In between, of course, we pray the prayers of our youth, words of comfort and tradition. But, immersed in the recitation of routine, even religious routine, there is little time for listening to what the Word of the universe might be trying to say to us.

The image the teacher uses is a simple one: Sometimes we can lower our heads over quiet waters and see into our own eyes. But when the waters roil, we find the image splintered and distorted. Nothing we see then can be trusted to be real. But more than that, when our souls are filled with noise, contemplation itself suffers. The noise of nothingness, the rattle and clamor of useless agendas, entombs us in ourselves. Then, contemplation itself is endangered. Distraction and ambition, anger and jealousy, pride and pain, fatigue and overload—all these distort the sense of the presence of God for us.

Scripture teaches that "God is not in the whirlwind." (1 Kings 19) And now again, in the third century and in our day and night, the monastics of the desert are clear: To rest in God we must learn to put out of sight and out of mind the whirlwind that threatens to engulf us. We are to allow contemplation to bring us home to the God of Life within us—the Life that exists everywhere else in the universe at the same time. Whatever it is that roars in us and separates us from the calm center of ourselves must go now. There the God who seeks us all our days waits for us to come wholly present to the Life that transcends the confusion of the present. Then nothing shall harm us, nothing frighten us, everything will give us peace. But only after the center is calm. Only after the noise within has died. Only after we have learned to listen to the God who speaks in the quiet of the centered soul.

As surely as this saying was important to the shift of cultures from the third to sixth centuries, even more so is it necessary to us. We are a people in transition from the local and the national to the global and the secular. No single institution is big enough to save either our individualism or the spiritual lives we must fashion within us, if, in fact, we are to come to know God at all.

For that, only the silence of our own souls will do—the personal connection between God and me.

Chapter Twenty-One

INTEGRITY AND LIBERATION

Abba John the Little said: "We have abandoned a light burden, namely self-criticism and taken up a heavy burden, namely self-justification."

T he opportunity to delude ourselves into thinking we have finally achieved a given level of spiritual maturity lurks everywhere in a world like ours. We are immersed in otherwise temporary measures of our sense of spiritual growth: how often we pray, how attached we are to a Church, how righteous we are. And, in the end, the damage it wreaks in us and around us is incalculable.

We assume that a special kind of maturity accompanies success. We look to those who sit upon the thrones of life as having earned them somehow. And so they become our mentors and our models. We accept their plans and applaud their positions. But nothing changes. The rich still exploit the poor. The selfish still ignore the needy. What kind of spiritual maturity is that? And what do we have in a world such as this that can possibly save us from it? Where will we cull the wisdom it takes to tell one kind of wisdom from another? What kind of power can save us from the powers that kill the soul and often even the body? We wander from guru to guru always seeking, perhaps, but never sure the way is true.

We take it for granted that years alone will bestow wisdom on a person. And so we ourselves do little to seek it since time itself will provide it for us. There will be time for that kind of concentration when the career path has ended, we think, and so we live now on the barest of spiritual touchstones: church membership, generous donations, the right amount of involvement at the right time.

We presume that power is a sign of internal worth and value—if we think separately of internal enrichment at all. In fact, all around us there are other directions to other kinds of life, equally enticing and even more clear: set your heart on great profit, they say, set your mind on public status. Set your life on what you control, they demand, and so we forget to ask ourselves what controls *us* instead.

We are certain that wealth and the privilege it brings must surely be signs of accomplishment, secular as well as spiritual. Indeed, the society in which we live is alive with signals that purport to separate us from childish notions of the spiritual life. But to become adult icons of spiritual growth, the Desert Monastics knew, was the exercise of a lifetime.

Abba John had no delusions about the nature of spiritual development. It comes, he teaches, from the standards to which we hold ourselves, by the efforts we make to be the best we can be, whatever the distance between our goals and our achievements. It is not measured by the excuses we give for not being the person we said we would be.

The spiritual life is not about self-justification: it is not about explaining why we are not the spiritual giants the world has a right to expect us to be. It's a matter of speaking the truth in a culture lived to lies. It means staying the course on behalf of the poor. It means refusing to back down when the oppressed, the marginalized, and women are simply ignored by the powerful and the wealthy. It is about having the courage to admit to ourselves those moments where we could have spoken out, spoken up, spoken on for those have no voice. It is about why we were silent when we could have, should have, spoken. It is a matter of asking ourselves, for whose favor did we prostitute our souls? Or, just as serious, for whom did we do good, not for their sake but for the approval of those whose favor we ourselves were seeking?

Abba John warns us: spiritual integrity is not about self-justification, the impossible burden of which exhausts the soul. It is about the liberation that comes from self-criticism. It is about being freed by self-criticism to go beyond the emptiness of the self to the point of stretching over and over again to be the self we were born to be.

Chapter Twenty-Two

SLOW SPIRITUALITY

A brother came to see Abba Theodore, and started to talk and inquire about things which he himself had not tried yet. The old man said to him: "You have not found a boat or put your gear into it, and you haven't even sailed, but you seem to have arrived in the city already! Well, do your work first; then you will come to the point you are talking about now."

I f there is anything that marks modern society, it is its addiction to speed. Read the ads: this compound produces radishes in half the time. This car goes from 0 to 60 mph in 9 seconds. This academic degree can be gotten in half the average time. This plane to Europe gets you there in time for dinner. Every year the internet gets faster. Every year racing yachts get built out of lighter material to fool the winds and ride the waves seconds faster than the boat next to them.

If truth be known, everything in this society is judged by the speed at which it can function in a fast-moving world. No machine, no skill, no discipline escapes the challenge. The goal of life is to get there faster than ever before. Life in our world has become a race to everywhere. Speed has become a sign of power, of superiority, of super human quality.

But not here. Not with Abba Theodore for a guide. There are some things worth doing, he teaches, that are worth doing slowly enough to learn from every facet of them. Like the spiritual life, for instance.

Most of us were born into a Church, a tradition, a world view, a theological mind-set, a family that brought us up "in the faith." But the religious affiliation was not "discovered" in situations like that. It was inherited. We simply were what we were: Catholic, Lutheran, Anglican, Evangelical. But there is more to faith than birthrights and buildings. It's not just worship times and adherence to the rules that keep us where we are. The truth is that as time goes by, at least for many, questions begin to plague the thinking seeker. And then the soul begins to throw off the trappings of religion in order to find and test the well from which the old answers sprang. In fact, if anything wages war on faith as we grow, it is surely a structure concentrated largely on worship times and adherence to the rules.

And so, when the questions come looking for answers to explain the reasons behind the worship and the purpose behind the rules, when the system itself is no longer holy enough to persuade, then the real work of the spiritual life can finally begin. Anything before this eye-opening phase of spiritual consciousness is purely preparatory, only grist for the mill of a life that seeks to be as spiritual as it is religious.

It's here that Abba Theodore slows the process down so that we might be shaped not by the quick-fix answers to the great questions of life but by the process of the search itself. He indicates three phases of the spiritual search, all of them slow, all of them a turning away from the secular self to a recognition of the Presence of God in the here and now.

The first dimension of the spiritual life, Abba Theodore is clear, is to want it, to choose the boat that will take you to the depths of the spirituality you seek. You must want to be at a point where the presence of God is a given but an untested reality in the seeker's own life. At that point, the seeker struggles to let go of anything and everything that either obstructs the felt presence of God in life or tempts the seeker to take it for granted. It takes hard work to dig out the great models of the faith and then to discover exactly what it was that made them great models in the first place. You must prepare the gear you'll need to make your way through the spiritual life. And that takes time. Time to study; time to reflect; time to choose.

Here speed is totally useless. An emerging consciousness of the Presence of God in the here and the now comes in slow, fleeting glimpses. Something here, my heart knows, is about and beyond what is to be expected in this situation: God is here. Something I never thought of happens, though no one takes credit for doing it: God is here. Somehow I am beginning to see beyond the obvious to the palpable love of the Creator for Creation. God is here. God is surely here.

And then the Abba says, "Well, do your work first; then you will come to the point you are talking about now." Life changes.

The slow, hard things of life simply bring more of the good. Of course, God is here. No, it does not come quickly, this vision of a world beyond the world. But soon, soon, it gets clearer—what I am seeing is more than only nature itself can unfold: Indeed, God is here. God has always been here. I have been here, too, but there have been the struggles of ambition, direction, and speed that blocked my vision.

It has all been worth the struggle for direction, the collection of gear, and the long sail to one day look up and know that the long struggle has been worth this coming to terms with the Life that lives in each of us. And once we're there, slow as the journey may have been, the stars within us, the stars we steer by, will never disappear again.

Chapter Twenty-Three

CAPITALISM AND CHRISTIANITY

It was said about one brother that when he had woven his baskets and put handles on them, he heard a monk next door saying: "What shall I do? The trader is coming but I don't have handles to put on my baskets!" Then he took the handles off his own baskets and brought them to his neighbor saying: "Look I have these left over. Why don't you put them on your baskets?" And he made his brother's work complete, as there was need, leaving his own unfinished.

I f the Desert Monastics have anything to say to the twenty-first century, it may well be this anonymous Saying that has us most in mind. The scene is a simple one: In the monastic economy of the time, monks did manual labor to provide for the necessities of life. Many made baskets out of hemp and then sold them to traveling traders who then recovered their money by selling the baskets at market. It was a society of retailers and wholesalers, a business model which exists to this day. At one level it's an efficient economic model. Everybody works and takes care of themselves. And the community thrives because everybody is thriving.

But that's not the whole picture. At another level, such an economic philosophy leaves an important question unanswered: What happens to people who can't produce enough baskets for the trader to sell? What happens to people with physical disabilities who can't get to market to sell them themselves? Where do the elderly fit in such a society? What happens if everybody doesn't work, cannot sell, or doesn't sell enough to see themselves through the down times? Who cares for whom then?

You would think that the Desert Monastics were dropped into the House and Senate of the United States where the question of who takes care of those who cannot take care of themselves threatens too commonly to divide the country. Why? Three elements of life concern modern society in ways the Desert Monastics simply eliminated out of hand. Capitalism rests on three principles—personal security, rugged individualism and means-testing. It's an "everyone for themselves" theology. In a society like this, we are all meant to take care of ourselves.

Modern society works with one thing in mind: personal security. We train every generation to work all their lives in order to have saved enough money to finance their needs for the rest of their nonworking lives. At one level, at least, it's a laudable goal. It speaks of personal responsibility and lifelong independence. The problem is that it also raises the question of community— its meaning and its obligations. It says quite clearly, "he took the handles off his own basket and brought them to his neighbor....he made his brother's work complete."

Our society also teaches rugged individualism—meaning total commitment to self. The heroes of a culture like this are the people who simply abandon the norms and needs of society to make as much money as they can, to assure the good life for themselves. The problem here, of course, is that without a common definition of the decent life, the entire community risks public diminishment without universal support. Then whatever the community seeks—bridges, highways, schools, housing projects, a basic quality of life for everyone—decays. Projects of this proportion are simply too major an operation either physically or financially to be universally restored by individuals acting alone.

Finally, to cement these elements of civilization, capitalist society resists the collection of taxes that make social services possible for everyone. Or worse, whatever surplus is available to the population at large is sparingly distributed. Charity begins to depend on means-testing—the determination of acceptable degrees of poverty, starvation, and illiteracy which qualify the indigent for support. Which is exactly where this Saying of the Desert Monastics interrupts the smooth-flowing current of political self-centeredness. For the sake of compassion, for the sake of human community—for all our sakes—it sets a different standard.

The monastic story couldn't be more obvious. Here, a monk hears the pain and plea of the one who has no resources. Why the basket handles are not done, we don't know. But we do know that the man is crushed for want of them. "What shall I do?" he cries.

And no answer is required. He does not need to prove that he will pay back the gift. He does not need to explain his errors. He is not left to fend for himself alone. Another monk steps in to make life right. The man is saved. The community is saved.

Too simple, you say? What is too simple about taking care of those who have worked all their lives and then find themselves facing the elements alone—without gas, without heat in the North and without electricity and air conditioning in the South? When there are thousands of jobs available but too few students who can read and write and think and compute well enough to apply for them, whose fault is it that the illiterate have not been put in the remedial classes that would make them employable?

It's a simple saying, indeed: One monk cries, another answers him without punishment or oppression. Security here is a direct response to need, as in, "Do unto others as you would have others do unto you." Community is built up by holding one another up. Means-testing is just one more way to take dignity, as well as resolve, away from a person. It labels them, categorizes them, limits their reach. In a world like this, poverty is the eternal divide between the successful and the failures. In a situation like this, it is those who doom the poor to begging, to humiliation, and to loss who are really the failures.

The cry of this chapter is not an old one. It's not an histor-ical anachronism. It is the eternal attempt to awaken the soul of those who confuse capitalism with Christianity yet today. It is a cry that has been heard clearly across the ages—from Roman colonies themselves to the Asian industries that have become the underpaid labor force of Western industries. It is the echo of the cries of feudalism, of the French Revolution, of the industrial era, of the era of agribusiness and now in a world where drones and robots and 3-D printing turn jobs into profit and skilled workers into day laborers.

If the question is, What could the Desert Monastics have to say to a world such as ours fifteen hundred years later? the answer is clear. In our era and in this culture, compassion, capitalism, and Christianity are just alike enough to be confused. Worse, they are just unlike enough to be careening toward a future in which none of them will survive without the other. If the story says anything, it is surely a cry from one age to another to examine each of them—alone and together—before Capitalism ruins the globe with its rampant profit taking; before compassion is confused with Christianity and people begin to see small donations as the answer in a world that needs a total overhaul of each; and before Christianity reduces itself to ritual—as it has so often done in history when it should have been the conscience of the world.

For the Desert Monastics, the resolution was a simple one, an obvious one, a communal one, a Christian one. The Saying concludes: "And he made his brother's work complete, as there was need, leaving his own unfinished."

Chapter Twenty-Four

THE SPINNING WHEEL OF SUCCESS

Saint Syncletica said: "Just as a treasure exposed is quickly spent, so also any virtue which becomes famous or well-publicized vanishes. Just as wax is quickly melted by fire, so the soul is emptied by praise and loses firmness of virtue."

A statement like this one may have struck a vein of serious spiritual depth in third-century Egypt. In the twenty-first century, however, Syncletica's rather casual dismissal of the importance of public acknowledgment of personal success could feel more like social churlishness, if not social discrimination.

In this culture in which, as Andy Warhol said, "Everybody wants their fifteen minutes of fame," the very thought of avoiding publicity seems like some kind of social treason. The idea now and here is to get more and more attention, to become more and more a center of attraction, however ephemeral the image may be. In the new global marketplace, publicity is key. The great commercial struggle is to capture all the light there is in order to become the light the world follows—for shoes or jeans or whatever. It is the opening of the self to a world of strangers.

And why? The reasons are legion, however mundane. And they make the point. Publicity converts to popularity, to influence, to outreach, to social support. And, if there is something to be bought or sold, established or developed, publicity converts to money, to precedence. Publicity is a winner-take-all game. To establish a monopoly on wisdom, to get a reputation for expertise, to build name recognition that can later be converted to money or political office or sales figures, is to become the flywheel of a movement: the supplier upon whose goodwill the local world depends and to whom society is indebted.

When the ad copy whirls across the TV screens in our living rooms every night, the implications of their ubiquity, their saturation levels, and their repetition escape us. It's all just the way things are: shallow, self-centered—and exhausted—by wanting more and more and more. We are part of the great public dance called the national economy. We are totally consumed trying to keep up with all the other publicity seekers around us.

It is the very situation Amma Syncletica defined centuries ago. Only then, she was warning the world—and even its Desert Monastics—about the danger of giving oneself away so totally that what is left is nothing but the husk of ourselves. Then, ironically, exhausted by the empty climb up the spinning wheel of success, we have become dry and lifeless, pale and uninviting. As our Novice Director warned us in the spirit of Syncletica long before our final profession, "My dear young sisters, remember this: the empty vessel must be filled."

The message is as important spiritually as it is physically. The message is a searing one: Once empty, the well of the soul is forever dry. Once the cultivation of the soul is ignored, the fruit of it can never, of itself, rise again. "The empty vessel must be filled." And the truth of it all was easily seen: When the soul is depleted, there is no more wisdom to give. There is no more depth to expect here than from any other to whom we have already given more than we can afford at the present time.

Once the principal of the treasure is touched, Syncletica warns us, it's so much easier to spend it all than to save it for another day. We treat the treasure like gold in a flowing stream. We do nothing to engender it, but we assume it will always be there. We're sure of its endless energy even as we're wearing ourselves out going spiritually and physically bankrupt.

Amma Syncletica's soul-vision is a true one. Even virtue, our special gifts and talents, she goes on, exposed too long, too much—more for show than in passion—will become too sapped to be revived again. We go through the steps of listening, counseling, and encouraging others, but we have lost the heart for it ourselves. Once forged in prayer and intent on responding to those in need, we are now in need ourselves. Worse, we are too far away from our own spiritual center to find our way back to where the heart hears best and the soul listens deeply. And yet it is only from the center of ourselves than we can possibly help the other.

"Just as wax is quickly melted by fire," she says, "so the soul is emptied by praise and loses firmness of virtue." Once the attention of the public settles on the strength that brings us to the height of ourselves, it is that very strength that is most in danger of collapse. The spiritual life is not about self-praise; the spiritual life is about being set on the Way, whatever the difficulty of the path, however hard the climb.

Does the spiritual word of an Amma in the third century have anything to say to us in our century? Only if you are an unusually skilled surgeon who is so much in demand that you haven't taken a month off in years. Only if you are the director of the local soup kitchen who does all the cooking yourself and, in the off hours, runs a food pantry on the side. Only if in the name of holiness, you have neglected your own spiritual life, your own physical energy. Then, it is clear that to be one of Amma Syncletica's disciples, it is time for you to stop for a while. Rest. Look at life again—this time through the vision of spiritual wholeness that started this work in you to begin with.

Chapter Twenty-Five

WHAT MAKES FOR SPIRITUAL TRANSFORMATION

Abba Poeman said to Abba Joseph, "Tell me how I can become a monk." And he replied, "If you want to find rest here and hereafter, say in every occasion, Who am I? and do not judge anyone."

I had never seen anything like it before. On a street corner of a major park in India he stood on one leg, unmoving, totally silent and dressed in what I suppose was the modern equivalent of "sackcloth and ashes." He was penance and holiness on display for all to see. His hair was gnarled and knotted, his feet were black, and his eyes bore through to the heart of every person who passed him by. Only the children, I noticed, gave him no notice at all. Somehow he had managed to exceed their definition of human—and so they simply ignored him or chased one another around his still, dark frame. They had no category in their heads for him and no way to make a place for him in society. A few idle looks and he became invisible thereafter.

This, I knew, was not an updated version of the Desert Monastics. No lines followed him for spiritual counsel; no group gathered around him in prayer. No Brothers in animal skins and bare feet joined him for Vespers as the sun grew gold and the night sky turned orange. Darkness bore down on the picnicking, strolling crowds, but he simply stood there. A reminder. But of what we did not know. Only one thing was clear: For some reason we simply did not meet the level of spiritual life to which he bore witness.

Since I myself had never seen another one of his types, I could not be sure exactly what kind of spiritual life he offered us. Instead, like the children, I felt no great attraction to him whatsoever. Nor did I feel guilty for things I must have done but could not identify. Indeed, this man, sincere as he could be, was too unlike my life to inspire me to leave my clothes behind and wait for everyone else to do the same. But what he did inspire in me was the urge to answer Abba Poeman's simple challenge: What is a monk, anyway? And how can I become one?

If the Desert Monastics were anything at all, they were single-minded, yes. But they were not the religious police of the Church. They were not the heralds of doom and spiritual fear in Egypt. They were not spiritual spies who spent their lives reporting on the moral mistakes of the people around them. They were not otherworldly creatures who stared into our hearts and found them wanting.

On the contrary. The Desert Monastics, history confirms, were simply centered in God. Sometimes they lived together in a kind of semi-community for support in their life's spiritual desires. Often, they spent their days in prayer and study, in discussion and holy silence. Sometimes, some of them performed great penances. But not always. And not as the sole public center of their lives. No, they were not the TV preachers of their day, nor even the great local confessors who frightened people back into the path of the straight and narrow. So, how did they become monks?

Abba Poeman was very direct about the level of sanctity cultivated at Scetis and its desert outposts: Every day say to yourself, Who am I? Think of the effect of a spiritual examen like that one: On Monday, Who am I? Answer: I am the one who is tired of staying here in the desert any longer. It's not anything like I thought it would be. On Tuesday, Who am I? Answer: I am the one who has little enough to give to the world but I would like to give it anyway. On Wednesday, Who am I? Answer: I am not that showoff who brings water to all of us every day. Who am I? Who am I? Who am I? At base, it is a simple enough question—but ask it often enough and answer it truthfully enough and you might, sometime, answer it sincerely enough to know the true answer the next time you look in the mirror: I am the person who pretends to care for people more than I really do. Or, I am the person who talks about the Scriptures but seldom really sits with them and takes them seriously. Or, I am exhausted being a person who is trying to be faithful to a daily practice—but is not. Or, I am the person who never tells the truth about my family or background, which means that I have learned to lie well.

Suddenly the answer to what makes for spiritual transformation becomes plain: I will really be a monk when I put down all my righteousness, am honest about myself, and never again judge another person. I will be a monk when I learn instead to ask myself how it is that I have forgotten my own sins, my high-toned goals, my corrupted motives. How is it that I have condemned so many and failed to notice that despite all my attachments to myself, I can still hear the heart of God calling to me? I am the one who has become honest about myself.

The effect is immediate. Indeed, "Then comes rest, here and hereafter." I am not agitated now at those whose life and values and personality and wants are different from mine. I am at peace with who I am. I am sure of who I am. I refuse to lie about myself in any way any longer. I no longer allow myself to wrangle with others, even internally. I have finally become a monk who judges no one and so knows now how great is the God who loves me—not because I am holy but because I am not—and because now I really know it.

I am free now. There is nothing anyone can say about me that I have not already admitted about myself. Abba Joseph has enabled me to accept who I am. I don't need to lie anymore. I am ready to grow again.

Rooted in Self-Control

Abba Poeman asked Abba Anthony: "What should I do?" And the old man said, "Do not be confident in your own righteousness. Do not worry about a thing once it's done. And control your tongue and your stomach."

T here are things to be gained in a youth culture—speed, enthusiasm, wonder, excitement—for which nothing else in society can substitute. It gives all of life a sense of movement, a taste of possibility, a feeling of newness. We watch their dances and hear the beat of the drums under our feet. We hear old melodies fade away in the background. We see the wild flailing, the abandonment, and know that we are seeing a new world unfold before our very eyes. Newness is the mantra now. Revolution is its cry.

But in its wake, there trails a touch of sadness, too. The assessment of what has been lost as well as gained in these great sweeping winds of change is the role of the elder in a changing world. With the elder comes a change of pace. Reflection and tradition weigh more in the moment than strategy, and experience is as much a factor as experimentation. It is the role of the elder in every era to cull the new from the old, the tried and true from the speculative.

Elders bring to bear a sense of history—of what does and doesn't work—to the fluid moment. They evaluate and ruminate and look for ways to honor both the new and the old. They do not divide society from itself. They weld roots to wings.

Nothing is clearer about the value of those relationships than this Saying between Abba Poeman and Abba Anthony. Abba Poeman was already a wisdom figure in Egypt, quite capable himself of giving counsel to many and certainly competent to make his own decisions. But when it came to making just such a decision, Poeman takes his question to Abba Anthony. And Anthony, a recognized and revered leader, takes the question seriously.

The eleventh degree of humility in the Rule of Benedict treats a situation like this quite specifically. "Do only those things sanctioned by the community," the sixth-century document reads. Take counsel. Listen. Seek direction. While moving ahead stay close to the kind of counsel that has strengthened the community in the past. Stay close to the spiritual well whose life-giving water has brought you to this point.

The value of this Saying is immeasurable. It is much more than an exciting new answer, the effects of which no one knows. It is a reaffirmation of spirituality based in experience, grounded in the wisdom of the elders, and rooted in self-control. "Do not," Abba Poeman is told, "be confident in your own righteousness." However right you may have been in the past remember that your tie to the community is your lifeline. Test everything here—no matter how often you have been right, let the community save you from ever being wrong.

A good many contemporary organizations might still be operational and thriving if there had been more testing of isolated ideas. Less arrogance from administrators who confused being Chief Operating Officer with always being right might well have saved good ideas from being adopted without enough consultation. More than one community could have profited from having fewer leaders who insisted that being in charge was a synonym for always knowing what to do.

No doubt about it: This Saying glows with humility, with wisdom, with discernment. Rather than the clash of Titans, the immovable minds of philosopher-types whose spiritual worldviews were in conflict—we see a model of harmony. Inscribed in our hearts is the picture of two elders, Abba Poeman and Abba Anthony, in search together for the will of God in each of their lives.

The answer to "What should I do?" is so simple, so common, so basic that all of us recognize the truth of it. What we must do, the two holy elders decide, is to control ourselves, for when there is no self-control we barter the loss of humanity. Simple.

First, products of tightly bonded village societies, they know well that sanctity requires that we learn to control our tongues. Evil lies in saying things about others—true or not—that might harm them. And so the Desert Monastics valued silence. Then, they tell us, we must learn to control our stomachs, as well. We must eat to live, not live to eat. We must, the holy ones know, refuse to engorge ourselves. To give in to food turns us soft and slow. It takes the edge off our thinking. It muddies our responses, and, most of all, it holds us captive to our own lassitude.

What should I do? Abba Poeman asks for us across the years, and the answers never change: Discipline your tongue. Control your stomach. And once you have taken a step in life, do not spend your life obsessing over it. Instead, learn from it and move on. The counsel is universal. In fact, where in our own lives and cultures would this kind of counsel not still be holy making?

Chapter Twenty-Seven

PEACE OF MIND

A brother who had been living among other brothers asked Abba Bessarian: "What should I do?" The old man replied, "Be silent and do not measure yourself against the others."

A s much as we'd like to have it be otherwise, life is not a straight line. Over and over again, we find ourselves having to choose one direction or another. But neither of them are certain. Neither option is inviting. Worse, each of them is demanding if for no other reason than that delay is not an option: It is time to move. The job has ended. The money has run out. The environment has turned toxic. Nothing here really works anymore. So now what? Do we settle down where we are or should we keep on looking? Somewhere else, perhaps. Anywhere else, perhaps. And if we keep on looking, what are we looking for?

The truth is that "What should I do?" is everybody's question. It is the universal agitation that comes to every life, sometimes over and over again until we get it right. But there is a spiritual problem implied in the answer that makes it impossible to address. It all depends on how you interpret the question. Is the person's real question, "What should I do to handle this?" or "What should I do now if not this?"

The Desert Masters clearly understood the problem. In dialog after dialog the question rises again. But the Desert Monastics, it seems, also knew better than to try to answer the question in any particular way. As in, "You should go to Thebes now."

The Desert Masters knew that seekers were not really asking someone else to choose the particular activity that might suit them best. On the contrary. The monastics spent their lives on issues far larger than that. They knew that the real answer depended first on helping each seeker to discover and articulate the real question. It was a matter of bringing the seekers to determine for themselves what had caused their hearts to falter and their commitment to pale.

In today's Saying, the situation is obvious: This seeker, a younger monk, it seems, has come a distance looking for spiritual direction from Abba Bessarian. But why? He has already been living in a community of monks where spiritual direction would surely have been more than available. He doesn't ask Bessarian if he can stay with this first community or go. He's not asking Bessarian if he should live in community with him as a cenobite or go off on his own as a hermit. There's nothing about the dialogue that reeks of urgency or serious moral confusion. So what is he asking?

It's Bessarian's answer that is the universal key to the universal question. Bessarian says to him, "Be silent and do not measure yourself against the others." Bessarian does what the Seeker should have done: he looks at what is going on inside himself and sees turmoil for its own sake. The kind we all stir up in ourselves so often. And then he pronounces the cure: "Be silent." Stop obsessing. Quit looking for the next big thing. Learn from what is in front of you.

Then, as if it weren't enough simply to stop the incessant dissatisfaction within us, Bessarian touches the global nerve in anxious people: If you want to be happy and calm, quiet and contented with life as you know it, stop comparing yourself to everyone else. Be silent and stop comparing yourself to others. The two quiet ideas come with the force of a thunder clap in the soul.

Be silent takes us into the center of ourselves. In that place, the toxins of public disapproval can take no root. They have no place in the soul of quiet where stillness lives. They simply rest in the womb of the self, attracting no clamor and allowing no conflict. Silence is the antidote to confusion, to self-doubt.

But then the second idea completely eclipses the first. Silence simply surrounds the self with walls of Plexiglas that none may invade and no one can interrupt. It is the second idea—the capacity for contentment—that makes the self an impenetrable planet, even from its own intrusions. Only by comparing ourselves to others do we have the data for disappointment. To refuse to give in to comparisons, we find ourselves enough for us.

Indeed, Abba Bessarian has ignored the questions by going straight to the answers that unmask them. The question "What should I do?" becomes "Be silent. Stop complaining. Don't spread discomfort. Don't compare yourself to others. Be grateful for what you are and what you have and what you do not have. Then, you will find that life—wherever it is, whatever it is—is more than enough for you.

So what happens to the young Seeker in this dialogue? No one cares, because everyone knows that it is we ourselves to whom the Desert Monastic is speaking. And now we know: Where we are is enough for us. There is no reason to move now, because we have found in ourselves the real threat to peace of mind. And more: Whomever we are with, our lives are fulfilled. Why? Because we never allow ourselves to be more than we are, and so we never make of others less than they are.

Chapter Twenty-Eight

GRACE AND SIMPLICITY

There was a man who was leading an ascetic life and not eating bread. He went to visit an old man. It happened that pilgrims also dropped by and the old man fixed a modest meal for them. When they sat together to eat, the Brother who was fasting picked up a single soaked pea and chewed it. When they arose from the table, the old man took the Brother aside and said: "Brother, when you go to visit somewhere, do not display your way of life, but if you want to keep to it, stay in your cell and never come out." He accepted what the old man said, and after that behaved like the others whenever he met with them.

I t happened on one of my early visits to England. I was a Westerner with an exalted sense of British history and a great love for the pomp and circumstance of it all. To walk streets where the kings and queens of England had walked was still a very, very heady brew. This was history alive and functioning; this was the living glory of glorious dynasties. And we were all a part of it yet. We were all being carried on the backs of greatness. Certainly such continuity gilded us all with the starlight of the past and the glow of a starched and proper present.

And then I heard the story that changed my mind about both culture and sanctity. It seems that at a great state dinner hosted by the queen, political commoners from every end of the globe sat sprinkled among the Royal Family. Unaccustomed to formal dining, they struggled with the multiple forks and spoons, water glasses, and wine goblets that characterize high society and public propriety. A particularly uncomfortable delegate to the left of the Prince played aimlessly with the small water dish by the side of his serving of oysters. Meant to rinse away the odor of fish on the user's fingers, it came with a piece of lemon and a small linen cloth. Suddenly, obviously nervous, the guest glanced, picked up the little finger bowl and drank it. The Prince sitting next to him and about to rinse off his fingers in his own little water dish hesitated for only a moment. Then he picked up his own finger bowl and, like the commoner before him, he drank it.

It was a gesture of ultimate humanity and genuine humility. The Prince did not embarrass the commoner; instead, he chose to become a commoner himself. It is the essence of good manners, he had been taught, that you do not make other people uncomfortable. Apocryphal as the story may be, it is nevertheless a call for the kind of humanity that characterizes the best of British society, from Westminster to Soho.

But the Desert Monastics know something the Prince did not. In this present Saying about holiness, the Desert Monastics tell us first what holiness is not. The old men of the desert, the wisdom figures of the time, know the difference between pseudo-sanctity and real holiness. Real holiness, the story is clear, never embarrasses the other. Nor lords it over others. Nor parades its religious symbols as badges of personal piety that are really indications of personal pride.

The lessons are timely yet. Even in societies that value pluralism and support interfaith activities, the tendency to compare our own religious festivals to the public religious identity of others remains a constant. But it's not our differences that measure our religious witness. It's what we do to make the world a better place together. Holiness is not about what we do to make ourselves the center of public attention as religious figures; it's about what we do for the people around us who need a figure of faith to support their own—whatever their denomination.

In this Word, the Desert Monastic's belief is embedded in the goodness of all the people in the community, not in religious hierarchy. The Holy One ignores the one who is busy showing off his holiness but identifies with the simplicity of the rest of the community.

Even more important for our own learning is the fact that the Master gives the ostentatious religious person a clear choice: stop posturing, or commit yourself to a hermitical lifestyle away from those who would be repulsed by thinking of religion as some kind of public extremism. To the Desert Monastic, religion was not a public exercise. It was a purely personal, totally internal pursuit of the spiritual life. To give oneself to a truly religious life was to seek wisdom, to become simple, to immerse oneself in the Word of God until it permeated every dimension of life.

But the bogus Desert Monastic in this Saying is an object lesson in what is not an authentic sense of commitment. This new monastic seeks public approval—even awe, perhaps. He intends to be an inspiration rather than a model. He sees the spiritual life as some kind of mime rather than a life-changing commitment. With that kind of plastic piety, he can never really become an authentic witness to anything but himself. It is an empty life, seeking self-aggrandizement. It has nothing to give to others of any depth, and it has no idea of what it means to become more than the self.

Here in this tale of the Desert Monastics, a religious posturer pretends to be simple in the house of those who are truly simple, and fails to see in them the authenticity he himself lacks. Only the old monk recognizes what is going on, and invites the public religious to leave the public community rather than mislead its sense of spirituality even more.

The story leaves us all asking two major questions: How much of me is really religious and not a pretender? And second: Am I sincere enough about anything to discover what I really have as well as what I really lack spiritually? Is it even possible for me to become a seeker who can concentrate on anything other than the self?

Chapter Twenty-Nine

THE PURPOSE OF WORK

An old man said: "I never wanted work that was useful to me but loss to my brother. For I have this expectation, that what helps my brother is fruitful for me."

I f there is anything that demonstrates the different mind-sets between the Desert Monastics and the modern world, this may well be it. In the twenty-first century, in our lifetime and in this culture, jobs become the center of life. What we do determines who we are—and whether or not what we're paid for doing is worth a life. We ask children as young as six years old what they want to do in life and why. We ask high school students to decide on college courses according to what work they hope to do when they get out of school. And, most of all, we link our definition of success to whether or not we will be paid for doing what we say we want to do.

As a result, some of our children grow up as engineers who will get in on the ground floor of the new companies who frack for gas, while others of our children will become lawyers who fight the development of fracking on the grounds that fracking affects the purity of the state's groundwater. For every interest, we create a counter-interest. We develop bankers who create hedge funds to increase borrowing. Then we create boards of government regulators who expose the false profits the borrowers are counting on. In fact, work is exactly what divides the modern community.

And yet, in a culture of Desert Monastics, all of whom live highly individualized spiritual lives, the basis of community—according to this Saying—is exactly the opposite. The monastic says, "I have never wanted work that was useful to me but loss to my brother." Today, the question of who or what will be hurt by the work I'm doing is yet to be part of the social conscience. Urban planning marks out residential areas and commercial zones in order to define and separate one from the other. But no one asks whether what is done in one part of town might not be threatening the lives or livelihoods of other people in that very same city.

To hear the Desert Monastic say, "I have this expectation that what helps my brother is fruitful for me" tears away the veil that makes it possible to hide the difference between profit and progress. The fact is that we learn early in an industrial world to think that whatever creates profit also enables progress.

Only one hundred years later do they tell us that coal dust caused black lung disease. And that nuclear weapons threaten all life on the planet. And that we have no intention of taxing coal mining in order to pay for the damage black lung disease caused to the people who mined it. Or, more to the point, we go on producing nuclear weapons despite the fact that we already have more than enough nuclear weapons to destroy all life on earth. We do not ask—though we do assume—that "what helps my brother is fruitful for me."

The results are obvious: Our lives are lived in the hope that our own choices are life-giving for others, but we have yet to accept the principle that what is not good for others—nuclearism, genetically modified farming, fossil fuels—is not fruitful for us, either.

The wisdom of the Desert Monastics about work is clearer in this century than it might have even been in their own time. It is time to prove to ourselves and others that the way we earn our own living is life-enhancing for others as well. "I never wanted work that was useful to me but loss to my brother," the old man says. Yet before that can ever be the situation again, we are all going to need to understand why we were created in the first place.

Clearly, the function of work is to complete the creation begun by God but meant to be completed by us. Yet, the planet is being farmed by the industrialized world to profit the industrialized world while African resources are being poached everywhere. Indian children are working for slave wages to clothe the children of the West. The seas are being fished out with little or no concern for their replenishment. And, all the while, the gifts of humanity are being spent on the degradation of creation.

The purpose of work is the care of the other. And the desert monastics have shown us how that can be—must be—done. Until the consciousness of the importance of my work to the development of the world is universal, we will all simply continue to work for our own good. Which, ironically, will be exactly the decision that destroys our own dreams as well everyone else's.

Chapter Thirty

OUR VALUES, OUR CHOICES

An old man said: "If you have lost gold or silver, you can find something in place of what you lost. However, if you lose time you cannot replace what you lost."

T his Saying of the Desert Monastics is centuries old, and yet the insight is surely as fresh today as it was when it was first collected as an example of uncommon wisdom. The question is, Why? After all, the early monastics lived in the center of the desert, outside the great cities of Egypt. Their lives were simple, even sparse. So how is it that they could be so cavalier about losing gold or silver?

The secret to what we'd grieve if we lost it lies more in what we value than in what we have. The old monastics of the desert didn't have silver or gold, no, but more than that, they simply didn't care about it to begin with. Like most of the rest of us, they cared for what they valued. And though things are worth whatever amount others ascribe to them, every item begins with an internal value. A thing is worth, in other words, whatever another person is willing to give up to get it. But it is also worth whatever we would give up to get it in the first place. I might be willing to give up sleep, perhaps. For something like the mortgage payments on a home, it might seem worth it to give up family time and take a second job. All the effort I'm willing to put into digging out diamonds, or panning for gold, has something to do with what I value—and what I do not.

Indeed the Desert Monastics did not value "things." They had actually, consciously, given up things ages ago. Instead, they valued the one thing that gave them the option to become whatever it was that they valued. What they really wanted was the time to become the best of whatever else life might challenge them to be.

In this culture, on the other hand, we seem to think that gold and silver, wealth and influence, are the answer to everything. We work hard to buy a summer house big enough to treat our children and entertain our friends. But by the time we're old enough to rest there ourselves, the kids are gone. The friends have moved away. And we learn something new: That this kind of rest doesn't much interest anyone anymore.

So what good are the gold and silver we own or count or collect? In what way, if any, do they give life value? Yes, gold and silver can get us new cars and a family trip across the United States and a lavish anniversary party. Better yet, we can exchange for more art or more land or a bigger apartment. But why? And then what? Who have we become by doing these things? What kind of person are we once all the treasures, all the commendations have been hung? What has happened to my life as a result of what I've done with my gold and silver? What happened to the marriage, to the kids, to the dreams I dreamed but never took the time to follow? To whom are we important now? Or, better yet, what has happened to my life because of all the time I've lost? Each part of it was meant to be another part of the fullness of me. And so much of it missing that it is too late to pursue now.

The questions are huge. They require us to see life as a whole rather than as a series of self-determined and isolated triumphs. They prod us to examine every element of life—the physical, the emotional, the social, the ethical, and the spiritual—and the effect of time on each of them. They obligate us to admit to ourselves what isn't happening in our lives because we have, at one level at least, chosen against it.

In our choice for gold and silver, the old men knew—for things rather than for the quality of life offered by a more human use of time—so much of life washes away unnoted and unused.

We work too hard and too long, to leave no time for a truly spiritual life and our own reflections on the kind of life we're living. Instead, life becomes a dash and a paycheck with little pause to determine what that is doing to us interiorly. Then we do even less of an audit of exactly how much our life might mean to the people around us if we did something else with it. Physically, we fail to understand that the deep fatigue and the loss of good order in our lives is a direct by-product of not allowing time for genuine rest and internal reflection. We feel life skew before we realize that we have backed ourselves into a corner and a cave of our own making.

When the psychological collapse finally comes—and it will—we find ourselves emotionally blind to the effects of stress. We lose track of the years when we gave every dimension of life a time and a place. We forget that life has a gift and a lesson for us to recognize and from which to take emotional direction, if we will only spend enough time on it. Socially, when we give ourselves over to one dimension of life, we lose control of what it means to live well on a daily basis. We cut out whole portions of life—new friends, new entertainment, new group projects—and run the risk of getting lonelier by the day. Then we may collect ribbons and plaques in numbers. But ribbons and plaques, statues and fame, have little or nothing to do with the really good life. Things—the gold and silver of life—may become business ventures, attractions, challenges and even a kind of public definition. But what happens to them, to us, when their time ends? How shall we define the time we spent on them. Important? To whom? And for what reason?

The wisdom of the Desert Monastics is both plain and painful: Be careful what you give your life to doing, they warn. In the end, it's the way we use time to develop every dimension of life that determines the value of our lives.

Chapter Thirty-One

THE SPIRITUAL DIMENSION OF WORDS

Abba James said: "We do not want words alone, for there are too many words among people today. What we need is action, for that is what we are looking for, not words which do not bear fruit."

O ut of a culture of silence eighteen hundred years ago comes a warning about words. Which makes sense, of course. After all, who else can we expect to be more conscious of the excess of words than those whose inclination is to bend the soul toward silence? But, at the same time, what can a world long gone possibly have to say to us now that the axle of the planet has tipped exactly upside down?

Now, in our culture, we are all about words. In fact, our world drowns in words everywhere. Words slide across ticker tapes on the bottom of our television screens. While we watch one thing, they demand our attention to tell us something else. When we take long drives through miles of pristine countryside, words clutter every major highway with cheap and tawdry billboards. They interrupt the most stunning natural scenes on earth with kitsch. Cartoon characters in scorching red-hot colors blank out the bend of the river. Raucous paints burst through the twilight skyline to say: "Jake's old-fashioned country flapjacks!—Next Exit." The evening shudders with the oafishness of it. Unlike the Desert Monastics, we are downright besieged by words.

Our question, then, is what is there to do in this century but surrender? Since there is no getting away from words, are we meant to take them all in? Or is it better to keep alert to them, for fear we miss the good ones? Or should we simply become so inured to words that eventually they fade into the background of life? And how will we be able to tell one class of words from another, the great ones from the bad, the important ones from the foolish?

Abba James is quick to make the distinction for us. He does not counsel people to ignore the words. On the contrary, he calls us to clear and discriminating discernment. He's not asking people to disregard or discount what they hear. He is actually asking people to pay much closer attention than they commonly do to the effects and purpose of words. He is calling people to realize the spiritual dimension of words. The way we respond to the words around us has, he says, as much to say about us as it does about the words themselves.

Words, he tells us, call for action. What we hear requires a response, or the words will fall on other ears, touch other hearts, shape other people's lives in ways that do more to distort than to develop. What we fail to respond to affects the world around us. Words are not without meaning, not without effect, not without spiritual value, not without social impact. And it is up to us to make words real—or reject them to make them go away.

The fact is that words are never what they may seem. Words obscure reality as well as clarify it. We call alcohol "entertainment," for instance, and defend its power to relax us. But when a couple drinks means out of control, less responsible, those words must be unmasked. When words hide the immorality of trafficking girls by calling it "adult entertainment," Abba James calls this society, as he did his, to action.

Words uplift but they can wound, too. When words are used to destroy the confidence of another, to ridicule them, to destroy their energy, we have slain the other's life as surely as with a weapon. When we allow words to be used in our presence in ways that reduce women to things and men to animals, when we hear them and say nothing in reply, we numb our souls and make words the engine of social destruction.

Words can whitewash evil and manipulate thought as easily as they can strip away the veils of dishonesty—the half-truths used to sell inferior goods or promote immoral behavior.

We called the practice of selling debt to multiple anonymous buyers "hedge funds"—as in funds that hid us from responsibility—and we brought the economy down. We called war "defense," but we now know that there is no such thing as defense from weapons aimed from half a world away. And we say we are only using them to destroy hardworking fathers, pregnant mothers, infant children in the name of nationalism, democracy, justice, and freedom, without even the grace to blush.

Indeed, Abba James speaks very clearly to us and our century, far more surely than he could ever have spoken to his own. He speaks to us from the depths of his ancient desert, into the sterility and barrenness of our own. But we are bogged down in money and oppression, lust and exploitation, the abuse of children and the despoliation of women everywhere—including on the streets of our own towns. And we use words—progress, success, equality, and fairness—to veil it.

Abba James asks us: What are you saying about it? And what are you doing to stop it? And our answer is...?

Chapter Thirty-Two

HOLY GENEROSITY

Abba Epiphanus said: "God sells righteousness very cheap to those who are eager to buy: namely, for a little piece of bread, worthless clothes, a cup of cold water and one coin."

P erhaps one of the most difficult questions for a modern Christian to answer is whether spirituality really has anything to do with modern life in a pluralistic world. Whether or not the spirituality of the Desert Monastics can be reconciled, for instance, with the spirituality articulated in Pope Leo XIII's social encyclicals. Or more directly yet: What does the spirituality of the Desert Monastics of the third through fifth centuries have to say to a world riven by poverty, threatened by nuclearism, and dealing with global starvation? After all, aren't those political issues rather than spiritual issues? And, if so, how can we as individuals seriously hope to influence their resolution?

For instance, the prospect of a world dependent on genetically modified seeds raises the question of global almsgiving. Non-reproducible seeds will make it impossible for the poor even to grow their own food as the global economy tips more and more to the technological West. Food itself will become a weapon as one part of the world has the power to withhold seeds from the other part of the world for the sake of political gain. What can a spiritual tradition over eighteen centuries old possibly have to say to situations such as this?

The Desert Monks lived in large part by making baskets which they then took to market and sold. Beyond that, people made pilgrimages to the desert to visit monastic communities and made donations to sustain them. Also, people passing monks on the roads shared their own bread baskets or their old clothes to see the monks through the seasons. People gave donations out of reverence for these holy beggars whose open-handed hospitality to others, despite their own limited resources, modeled holy generosity. More than that, their commitment to personal poverty was itself a shining sign of dependence on God and freedom from enslavement to the things of this world. The monks sustained the people spiritually, and the people sustained the monks physically. It was a happy marriage of service and support.

In a sense, these things still go on in our own time. Monastic communities receive donations to this day, and then share them with all the others who crowd their doorways for shelter or depend on their soup kitchens. The unemployed indigent—too uneducated to operate computers—stand between the lanes of cars on our streets and hold signs that say, "Will work for food," or play pennywhistles in entrances to shopping malls to earn their way through life. There is never enough in the private community to feed them all.

The fact is that almsgiving has always been a fundamental mark of real religion. The world was made for everyone, the great religious argued, and everyone must receive their share. The earth yields enough for everyone. Therefore, we are all expected to see that those who cannot sustain themselves nevertheless receive what it takes to live a decent life.

God, Abba Epiphanus, is clear, rewards the givers. It is a small enough price, he comments, to pay for righteousness with so little an investment: a bit of food, some old clothes, a coin. Indeed. But beggars then and beggars now have changed over the ages. As have their almsgivers.

Beggars then had little less than the majority of the people who shared their foods with them. Those with more gave to those with less so that all could have enough. Beggars now, refused on every hand, live in shame in empty rooms or stand in long lines to beg crumbs from the richest government bureaus in the world. Those who live by begging now know the rest of us better than most. They know when, in silk suits, we throw some change in a beggar's box how really caring we are. They know we resent the food stamps they get. They know that the so-called minimum wage that hires people full-time for part-time wages makes it impossible for them to support their families, however hard they try. And they know that such policies make beggars out of workers— a truth that their better-heeled citizens and their wealthy governments refuse to acknowledge.

The question, of course, is whether or not such scantiness today really does buy righteousness in a world where to be part of the upper 1 percent of the population in Pennsylvania, for instance, Google says would be necessary to earn $355,000 dollars a year. In California, that number would be $540,000. Then, the small coins of the 1%, the 5%, the 25%, the 50% clink hollow against the begging bowl. Better the gift of the old widow than the watered-down charity of the passing rich.

The Desert Monastics leave us with such searing questions all these years later: Is it righteousness we're talking about when we toss a coin or two in the bowl as we pass? Or is it show? Or guilt? Or is it simply annoyance that those who have nothing have done nowhere near as well as we have ourselves? Why is that? Is it because they're lazy? Because they like to beg? Because it's a good living? Because we ourselves have never lobbied for a higher minimum wage, have done nothing to help them feed their children and pay their electric bills to keep the cold away.

Meanwhile, we hear that 3,300 people sleep on the streets of New York City every cold night. Even more people sleep in unheated, unfurnished apartments in every town and city in the so-called developed—meaning affluent—world.

What shall we do to stop Abba Epiphanus from haunting us these days? Is the little we do a sufficient price to pay for the righteousness we say we seek—the same righteousness we tell ourselves with confidence that we have? Is such paucity enough to save the rest of the globe from destitution and us from the righteous wrath of God?

Surely the Desert Monastics have set the standard high.

Chapter Thirty-Three

POWER AND PACIFISM

There were two old men who had lived together for many years and they had never quarreled. Now one of them said: "Let us try to quarrel once just like other people do." And the other replied: "I don't know how a quarrel happens." Then the first one said: "Look, I put a brick between us and I say, 'This is mine,' and you say, 'No, it's mine,' and after that a quarrel begins." So they placed a brick between them, and one of them said: "This is mine," and the other said, "No, it's mine." And he replied: "Indeed, it's all yours, so take it away with you!" And they went away unable to fight with each other.

O ver the years, in the face of world wars and international efforts at holocaust, humans have concentrated on the study of human relations. Scholars have gathered and analyzed information from every level of human endeavor—personal, organizational and international. The characteristics of human communication and the nature and resolution of human conflict have concentrated the attention of researchers around the globe. Few other social disciplines have claimed as much attention as this one.

The irony of the situation lies in the fact that spiritual disci-plines have also brought considerable attention to the capacity of the human being to exercise emotional control in human interac-tions. Nevertheless, religious ideals have not eliminated violence. In fact, the hope of being able to control the degree of human and social damage done in the name of national and domestic tensions at this point appears slim. Religious training, however, has been able to assert the moral dimensions of human behavior, and thus the standard of peace, as an essential quality of the reli-gious person. Even the Desert Monastics, separated from the civic institution and almost totally independent of even religious regi-mens, looked at the subject.

In this story of the experience of two Desert Monastics, four simple and basic spiritual principles emerge in an attempt to teach what it takes to become a pacifist presence in the life of the early Christian community.

In the first scene, the situation is clear: Peace must be taught. The two old men, wisdom figures of the monastic community, after having lived years together, simply did not know how to argue. They had never lived in a situation where argument was the *lingua franca* of victory or negotiation. Having lived where the character of the environment around them had been peaceful did not prepare them to use either force or litigation. They simply did not know how to engage in verbal sparring, let alone domina-tion, interruption, shrieking, roaring or caterwauling. They had not seen it done. They had no models of how to do it. They had not absorbed the fine art of emotional manipulation. The notion of behaving less than rational, the idea of attacking another for the sake of inducing an early surrender, the possibility of staging an emotional breakdown to weigh the histrionics in their own favor, was out of the question.

In the second scene, what history has proved as the essence of most arguments is defused. One old man simply refuses to lay claim to what is not his. He does not claim his right to something that no more belonged to him than it did to his brother. In fact, neither old man asserts a dishonest claim to the goods that might just as easily belong to the other. When the second old man agrees to relinquish the claim on which an argument would need to be based, there is simply no foundation for disagreement. He knew that he himself had no right to contend for the brick. And he didn't. Whether or not there might be someone else with a just claim was now irrelevant. This disagreement, at least, was baseless. And so, he had nothing to fight about. The learning is obvious. To refuse to argue, to refuse to pick sides—no matter who tries to fan the fire or to wants to make a case where no case exists—disarms the world.

In the third scene, the science of warfare is embarrassingly obvious: conflict is not necessary if no one wants to fight. Fighting is something we choose to do; it is not what we must do. We can, of course, walk away from struggles that will only lose more than they gain.

Finally, the old men teach, struggle can be stopped. In the very midst of the situation, we can just turn the stakes over to the one who claims them and choose another way to pursue the matter— like the French who allowed the Germans to take over the country in World War II, and then secretly worked to undermine everything they did. In quiet, secret ways, the powerless have another kind of power.

The Desert Monastics are strikingly strong here. What is certain is that violence is not necessary and that the nonviolent side is never really powerless. The question is: What kind of world do you want to build? What kind of power do you want to be known for? What kind of power will you yield?

Chapter Thirty-Four

WHAT IS HOLINESS?

A brother said to an old man: "There are two brothers. One of them stays in his cell quietly, fasting for six days at a time, and imposing on himself a good deal of discipline, and the other serves the sick. Which one of them is more acceptable to God?" The old man replied: "Even if the brother who fasts six days were to hang himself by the nose, he could not equal the one who serves the sick."

T his Word is about what it takes to be truly religious. The Word the Desert Masters leave us with here is a basic one, a conclusive one. In the first place, it is a Word from an old man—one of the long-time wisdom figures of the desert. Someone who has lived the monastic life for years. Someone faithful to its purpose. Someone who was clearly a sign of its value. Someone from whom others sought spiritual direction. Someone like this young brother in the story who was new to the spiritual life and seeking to see its path—as we all do.

The young brother's question is a standard one yet, centuries later. He embeds it in the story of two other young brothers: One fasts six days at a time and leads a highly disciplined life—he keeps a regular schedule, he doesn't miss prayer time, he never avoids his scripture reading. He is the very model of religious ideals. The first is a model religious. All we know about the second brother, though, is that he serves the sick. No mention of schedules or fasts. Which brother is more acceptable to God, the young man asks?

What's best spiritually, we all want to know, as we choose our life models. A life of spiritual discipline and ascetic practices, or a life spent caring for the needs of others but, apparently, a little lax about our own needs?

The old man wastes no time dawdling over the answer. About this question he has no doubt. His answer to the young disciple brooks no misunderstanding. No amount of personal fasting, he says, will save us. No measure of personal asceticism will gild our soul. "Even if the brother who fasts six days were to hang himself by the nose," he insists, "he doesn't begin to equal the one who serves the sick."

What are we hearing here? The question is clear: When it's all over, when we have said our last rosary, made our final trip to church, made our last private retreat, said the last of our prayers, fasted every day of our last Lent, and hung by our nose from the steeple of the church as a sign of our eternal commitment to God, will it have been enough to qualify us as saintly?

Only the old man says, if we spent our lives taking care of those who could not take care of themselves. Why? Because this is the Word that most echoes the life of Jesus, upon which the monastics' life is all about. The Desert Monastics follow the Jesus who walks from Galilee to Jerusalem curing the sick, raising the dead, and contesting with those along the way who would say that keeping the Law is greater than addressing the needs of the people.

But who are they? Who? They are the old woman across the street too weak to cook her own dinner. Who? The child with no family at home to take care of her after school. Who? The mother whose son is in jail for murder. Who? The cold who live on the streets during the winter. Who? The poor women in jail who have no money to get a lawyer. Who? The ill. The abandoned. The lonely. The destitute. Anyone who needs us over and over again because there is no one else there to care for them. That, the old man says, is holiness. It is that holiness that ought to be the fruit of all our religious practices. And it cannot be substituted for by "playing holy" for all to see while living only for ourselves.

"Abba, give us a Word," the disciples cry. And the Word that comes back is this one: Don't think that the spiritual life is about the self. It is a hard Word. But it is the only Word that counts.

The fact is that the only purpose for the spiritual life, the Desert Monastics tell us to this day, is to begin to see the world as God sees the world. It is about becoming the self that sees life through the eyes of Jesus and then, like Jesus, bends to become the miracle the world awaits.

Chapter Thirty-Five

BE COMPLETELY TURNED INTO FIRE!

Abba Lot went to see Abba Joseph and said: "Abba, as much as I am able I practice my little Rule, keep my little fasts, do my prayers and meditation, remain quiet and, as much as possible, I keep my thoughts clean. What else should I do?" Then the old man stood up and stretched out his hands toward heaven. His fingers became like ten torches of flame. And he said: "Why not be turned completely into fire?"

T he spiritual life, like so many other things in life, is lived in stages. And, ironically, it is not about going up to a higher realm of the spiritual life; it is about coming down to where we're meant to be in life. "We ascend by humility," as the ancients say, and we descend by pride. We grow closer to what we're supposed to be by becoming more our true, our real selves and less the carbon copy of a sixteenth-century ascetic or a nineteenth-century clerical potentate. Abba Lot got it all wrong.

But if we stay close to reality, we learn sooner or later that we are not in pursuit of a higher path to a higher life. We are, instead, on a very winding road that goes nowhere certain, but everywhere there is the need for me—for my real care, genuine presence, honest humility and absolute commitment to becoming the presence of God wherever I am.

The problem is that it can take years to understand the implications of words like that. We start young, most of us, and we believe everything they tell us: These are the rules; those are the sins. Here are the practices, the prayers, the disciplines, the traditions. Keep them. There are the models to follow and the cautions to keep in mind and the pitfalls to avoid and, of course, the prescriptions to keep at all costs.

But the spiritual life is not a program. Although a program—if it is right for the person, if it fits the personality and enlivens the soul—may certainly launch a person on a path of perfection. But oddly enough, the spiritual life is not about perfection. It is about the direction of the mind, the orientation of the soul, and the beat of the heart.

Instead of being a military regimen that concentrates the mind and exercises the body, the spiritual life captivates the soul of the person to such an extent that all of life becomes one's spiritual path. It leads a person with unfailing energy to what becomes the source of a person's life—and the only reason clear enough and enthralling enough to get a person up in the morning. We grow in insight. We develop in understanding. We advance in wisdom. And there comes a point where cautious consideration, tentative steps, and ordered behaviors are not enough. There comes a time when the spiritual life is more than a program of spiritual exercises. It is the whole-souled plunge into life; a life lived from a spiritual perspective, through the eyes of the poor and the needy.

Then, we stop worrying, "What will people think," when we speak out against the country's continuing participation in the latest war. We speak out for subsidized day care. We quit worrying about whether a couple in our church's book discussion group is heterosexual or homosexual. We quit fretting about whether men—or women—preach the homily as long as it opens my eyes about Jesus. We join an interfaith group as a commitment to world peace. We become totally human and loving. Most of all, we start to view all of life through the filter of the Gospels, the beatitudes, and through a commitment to peace and justice for all. We become less and less any kind of political partisans, and more and more Christian citizens of the world. We become a real Christian—but more than just Christian. We become totally American but more than just Americans. We refuse to be either anti-male or smugly sexist. Instead, we become "completely turned into fire."

Now, it is the light of God by which we walk. We are not bellicose and conservative Christians. We are not chauvinist citizens or redneck patriots. We are not righteous progressives. We have become like those Desert Monastics who will not count the sins of others, only their own sins. We are like those Desert Monastics who have little to live on themselves but go on giving to those who have even less. We are like those Desert Monastics who will break a rule to save a person rather than keep the rule and lose their own souls by preferring false righteousness to real sanctity.

At that point, all the fasts and prayers, all the disciplines and rules, have done what they were meant to do. They have prepared us to forget them when necessary and so become *real* religious. They have turned over the hard soil of our hearts. They have turned our stony hearts into hearts of flesh.

Yes, all the religious practices and traditions, the feasts and fervent devotions, have done their work. No, they have not made us great purveyors of the history of the tradition, nor keepers of its most arcane penances. Instead, they have stamped on our souls the soft outline of the caring face of Jesus. Now, whomever we touch will see that soft and loving look of Jesus.